The Middle School

THE LIBRARY OF EDUCATION

A Project of The Center for Applied Research in Education, Inc.

G. R. Gottschalk, Director

Categories of Coverage

I	II	III
Curriculum and Teaching	Administration, Organization, and Finance	Psychology for Educators

IV	V	VI
History, Philosophy, and Social Foundations	Professional Skills	Educational Institutions

The Middle School

DONALD H. EICHHORN

Assistant Supervising Principal,
Upper St. Clair
Township School District
Pittsburgh, Pennsylvania

The Center for Applied Research in Education, Inc.
New York

Foreword

Currently one of the most fashionable words on the educational scene is "innovation." This writer much prefers the term "improvement" because this concept, unlike "innovation," embraces not mere change but change *for the better*. Implicit in the concept of improvement is the necessity for making values and purposes explicit and for assessing proposed change against these values and purposes. Many innovations in education are not demonstrably improvements. Many are fads without adequate rationale in value and purpose; many are changes in form without substantial improvement in substance.

In this volume Dr. Eichhorn has faced the difficult but essential task of applying rational inquiry to one of the most promising improvements in school organization—the non-graded middle school. After scholarly examination of appropriate philosophical, social, and psychological foundations of the education for the prepubescent, the author has conceptualized a model of the middle school, pedagogically sound, administratively feasible (when resources are adequate), and well described. He has undergirded the middle school concept with a sound rationale and has set up an idealized model which contributes substantially to our acceptance of the middle school as an improvement rather than a mere innovation. Hopefully, the author's model will help the middle school find its destiny, both in concept and in practice, far better than its predecessor, the junior high school, did.

Interestingly, the author has accomplished all of this without demonstration grants, surveys of normative practice, or exhortation of the innovators, but by means of an exceptionally well formulated doctoral dissertation.

Dr. Eichhorn's credentials for this assignment are impressive. He is not only a thoughtful scholar but he is also the prime architect and acting administrator of a fine middle school working model in his own school system.

This volume will be helpful to practitioners working in middle schools and to the general reader who is interested in gaining a deeper understanding of this intriguing educational improvement.

RICHARD WYNN
Professor of Education
University of Pittsburgh

The Middle School

Donald H. Eichhorn

American schools have responded to changes in society and to differing needs of students in many ways. Basic structural changes are often involved. It was in such a manner that the junior high school came into being. The structural change presently being considered is the middle school. Donald H. Eichhorn has written a comprehensive description and analysis and in this volume presents a functional model of a nongraded middle school.

Dr. Eichhorn reviewed appropriate literature in psychology, sociology, the foundations of education, and educational administration. Concluding that children now mature more rapidly than those who lived earlier in the century, that social interest patterns develop at an earlier age, that social peer interaction patterns also develop earlier, that conventionally organized elementary and secondary schools do not take these changes sufficiently into account, he postulates that a new structure—a nongraded middle school—offers an opportunity to reorganize in such a manner as to offer children an education more appropriate for the present age.

The organization which Eichhorn recommends is a 5–3–4 plan with the possibility that grade 12 be the first year of junior college. The concept upon which the middle school is built is transescence, that is, the period in human development which begins in late childhood, prior to the onset of puberty, and which extends through the early stages of adolescence. It is for the transescents that the middle school is designed.

The proposed school is not a mere mechanical rearrangement of grades, but is a careful integration of an educational program resulting from cultural forces, mental, emotional, and physical growth factors, together with administrative variables, guidance activities, and teaching requirements. The middle school is seen as an organic whole with all of the relevant factors focusing upon the growth of the child.

Eichhorn's volume is worthy of careful study by all school practitioners. Certainly it presents a wide range of documentation supporting this new concept of school organization which appears to be gaining favor in this country. After studying this volume, the reader will be in a better position to determine the wisdom of this trend.

DANIEL E. GRIFFITHS
Content Editor

Contents

CHAPTER I

The Emerging Middle School   1

CHAPTER II

Physical Growth   7

Physical Growth   8
Growth Trends   9
Sexual Development   11
Earlier Sexual Maturation   12
Variables Affecting Maturation   14
Emotional and Social Implications of Maturation   17
Physical Efficiency   21
Implication for Education   22

CHAPTER III

Mental Growth   24

Intellectual Nature of Transescence   24
Characteristics of Stage Development   29
Variables Affecting Intellectual Growth   32
Implications for Education   37

CHAPTER IV

Cultural Forces   40

The Family and the Transescent   42
The Culture and the Transescent   48
Implications for Education   56

CHAPTER V

Middle School Environment   58

*Environmental Guideposts: The Relationship of
    Transescents' Physical Growth with the Middle
    School Environment*   59

Environmental Guideposts: The Relationship of
Transescents' Mental Growth with the Middle
School Environment   60
Environmental Guideposts: The Relationship of
Cultural Forces with Transescence in the Middle
School Environment   62

CHAPTER VI

Educational Program   65

Middle School Curricula   66
Physical-Cultural Curriculum   67
Analytical Curriculum   72
Middle School Grouping Considerations   77
Middle School Grouping Procedure   78
Analytical Grouping   80
Physical-Cultural Grouping   81
Professional Staff Relationships   83

CHAPTER VII

Guidance Services and Activities   86

Related Guidance Programs   87

CHAPTER VIII

Administration   91

Staff-Personnel Relations   91
School-Community Relations   94
Physical Plant   95
Fiscal Considerations   97
Evaluation   99

CHAPTER IX

Conclusions and Recommendations   102

Glossary   107

Bibliography   109

Index   113

The Middle School

CHAPTER I

The Emerging Middle School

Education in the latter decades of the twentieth century faces serious challenges. Underlying these challenges are elements of a constant and accelerating change taking place in technology, in human growth and development, in sociological structures and in expanding knowledge. While these developments have a profound effect on society in general, their impact on education is especially significant. Formerly established patterns of graded organizations, curricular programs and pedagogy seem unable to cope with the dynamic and complex societal needs of today.

Due to cultural factors physical maturation is occurring in individuals at an earlier chronological age than formerly; this trend is accompanied by similar trends in social interests. It is characteristic of American education to develop organizational patterns commensurate with the nature of its students; the current status of human growth and development suggests there is a definite need for designing a middle school to be based on the compatible physical and social traits of the students.

A school organization emerging out of cultural change is not unique in American education. The philosophical base of the junior high school developed as a result of diverse pressures. In this regard, Lounsbury[1] states:

> In some instances, even the champions of the junior high school movement came from different philosophical camps. College men advocated reorganization for economy of time. Public school leaders were concerned over better meeting immediate needs and saw the junior high school as a mean of doing this. Board of education members may have seen reorganization as an economy move, while teachers may have supported reorganization because it would bring about new and improved special facilities such as science laboratories.

---

[1] John H. Lounsbury, "How the Junior High School Came To Be," *Educational Leadership,* XVIII (December, 1960), 147.

1

At the beginning of the twentieth century another major influence leading to the growth of the junior high school was G. Stanley Hall's studies. These studies influenced Americans into believing that education should be based on psychology and that adolescence should be given scientific study.

All concerns—administrative costs, elimination studies, the concept of adolescent differences—provided the spark igniting the junior high school movement. In the decades following, the junior high school served American education with distinction. It firmly established the fact that there is a need for a transitional organization between the elementary and the high school levels, one which helps meet the physical, mental, and social needs of youngsters.

Since the inception of the junior high school, significant trends in human growth and development and changes in American culture have produced deep implications as to what the nature of this transitional school should be. Today's youth interacts appreciably differently with society than its counterpart did in 1900 as a result of this dramatic trend toward earlier physical maturation coupled with the marked cultural changes that have taken place over the past sixty year period.

As one views certain factors in the status of education today as it relates to society—(1) what society demands and expects of its youth, (2) what society demands in a two way educational movement (an acceleration in advanced placement courses and a downward movement in subject matter), and (3) a growing dissatisfaction with present junior high school programs—the situation brings conditions analogous to those which generated the junior high school.

Certainly many school districts are attempting various solutions through graded changes from the 6–3–3 organization. One example is the Fort Couch Middle School in Upper St. Clair, Pennsylvania. Dr. Carl R. Streams, supervising principal at the time the 6–7–8 program was founded, stated in a letter to the Pennsylvania Department of Instruction on August 25, 1959:

> We are requesting that the school be composed of grades 6–7–8.
> The reasons why we believe that this program is desirable and educationally sound are as follows:
>   1. From the physical and psychological point of view it is a more natural grouping. There appears to be less of a differential in

maturity between the sixth and eighth grade than between the seventh and the ninth grade.

2. The social patterns are more nearly the same in grades 6, 7, and 8 than in the conventional pattern of grades 7, 8, and 9. The social maturity of the ninth grade student more nearly parallels that of the older students. At the present time the ninth grade sets the pattern which is too advanced for the younger students. A better social program could be carried on without the ninth grade student.

3. The transition from the self-contained classroom to a departmentalized program may be more gradual. . . .

As it relates to the middle school, considering the nature of the youngster involved is vital. There is no precise term which can be applied. To state that all youngsters in the proposed middle school are prepubescents, early adolescents or adolescents can not be justified. In reality, the transitional school contains boys and girls from all these designations. For clarification purposes, the term transescent will be used to describe middle school youngsters and the term transescence will be applied to their stage of development.

Transescence: the stage of development which begins prior to the onset of puberty and extends through the early stages of adolescence. Since puberty does not occur for all precisely at the same chronological age in human development, the transescent designation is based on the many physical, social, emotional, and intellectual changes in body chemistry that appear prior to the puberty cycle to the time in which the body gains a practical degree of stabilization over these complex pubescent changes.

This writing will use a system-theory as a model to conceptualize a functional middle school. Primary considerations in the use of this approach are the definitions and relationships of system-theory and model. Griffiths[2] describes system-theory in this manner, "A 'system' is simply defined as a complex of elements in mutual interaction. System is a construct which has been used for a long period of time."

The fact that a grouping of students comprises a social system is described by Havighurst and Neugarten:[3]

---

[2] Daniel E. Griffiths, "Some Assumptions Underlying the Use of Models in Research" in *Educational Research: New Perspectives,* ed. Jack A. Culbertson and Stephen P. Henchely (Danville, Ill.: The Interstate Printers and Publishers Inc., 1963), p. 129.

[3] Robert J. Havighurst and Bernice L. Neugarten, *Society and Education* (Boston: Allyn and Bacon, Inc., 1957), p. 181.

The school may be viewed as a social system in much the same way as the family or peer group. Like the family or the peer group, the school acts as one of society's agents in socializing the child and in transmitting the culture. Also like the family or the peer group, the school has a subculture of its own—a complex set of beliefs, values and traditions, ways of thinking and behaving—that differentiate it from other social institutions.

The system-theory once defined will serve as the basis for conceptualization of a functional middle school model. Allport[4] extends the definition of the system-theory by stating:

> . . . any recognizably delimited aggregate of dynamic elements that are in some way interconnected and interdependent and that continue to operate together according to certain laws and in such a way as to produce some characteristic total effect. A system, in other words, is something that is concerned with some kind of activity and preserves a kind of integration and unity; and a particular system can be recognized as distinct from other systems to which, however, it may be dynamically related. Systems may be complex; they may be made up of interdependent subsystems, each of which, though less autonomous than the entire aggregate, is nevertheless fairly distinguishable in operation.

The aggregate of dynamic elements in this case are the mental, emotional, physical, and cultural relationships existing among middle school students. These elements are, by the nature of the school setting, interconnected and interdependent, and, although a part of a larger more complex aggregate system, are also fairly distinguishable in operation. The system-theory thus developed will be termed a socio-psychological model.

At this point, it is appropriate to discuss the term model as it is intended to be used. Since the purpose of this approach is to create a functional middle school model based on a system-theory, it is mandatory that a relationship be developed between the system-theory and the functional middle school.

The definition for model is succinctly given by Tyler[5] who states: "When an area about which we already know a good deal is used to suggest laws for an area about which little is known, then the fa-

---

4 Floyd H. Allport, *Theories of Perception and the Concept of Structure* (New York: John Wiley and Sons Inc., 1955), p. 469.

5 Ralph W. Tyler, "The Contributions of the Behavioral Science in Educational Research" in *First Annual Phi Delta Kappa Symposium on Educational Research,* ed. Frank W. Banghart (Bloomington, Ind.: Phi Delta Kappa, 1960).

miliar area providing the form of the laws may be called a model for the new area."

A property necessary for using a model in this context is the property of isomorphism. Griffiths[6] describes this property in this way:

> If X is a model of Y, it is so because X is isomorphic to Y. Two conditions are necessary for this to obtain. First, there must be a one-to-one relationship between elements of X and the elements of Y. Second, the elements of X must bear the same relationship to one another as do the elements of Y. If all of the elements bear the same relationship to one another, then the isomorphism is complete.

Brodbeck,[7] a leading analyst of the model research approach, extends the isomorphic discussion by relating the following:

> In other words, not only must the terms of the two areas correspond, but the connections among these concepts must also be preserved, if the model is to be of any use. One area, either part or all of it, can be a fruitful model for another only if corresponding concepts of the model also can be shown to connect their corresponding concepts in the second area.

The relationship as it applies to the model structures of this monograph is schematically illustrated in Figure 1 and will be developed in subsequent chapters. In designing the socio-psychological model, heavy emphasis is placed on related literature and on research findings relative to transescent behavior. The middle school model will be conceptualized based upon the elements of the socio-psychological model.

---

6 Griffiths, *op. cit.,* p. 123.

7 May Brodbeck, "Logic and Scientific Method in Research on Teaching" in *Handbook of Research on Teaching,* ed. N. L. Gage (Chicago: Rand McNally and Company, 1963), p. 90.

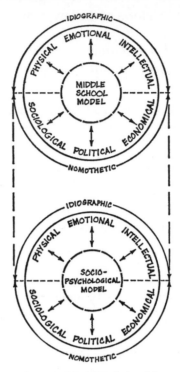

Figure 1. Model Relationship.

CHAPTER II

Physical Growth

In viewing transescents, one must consider the forces involved in their lives. There are two basic interrelated dimensions affecting the individual. First, there are forces from within, caused by internal body changes, which affects the child's relations with the environment. Conversely, there are external forces, generated by the environment, which impinge on the individual. These two dimensions form an inter-related socio-psychological model which may be used as a foundation when planning an educational program for transescents. Schematically, these two basic dimensions and their interrelated component parts are illustrated in Figure 2.

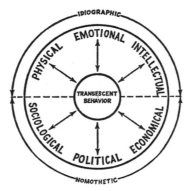

Figure 2. Socio-psychological Model.

The importance of the component parts of the socio-psychological model is emphasized by Strang[1] who writes:

> Facts about the physical growth preceding and following puberty are important for a number of reasons. Bodily changes, especially if sudden, change the adolescent's body image and self concept; he may now see himself as an adult with adult privileges and responsibilities. Biological changes give rise to physical sensations; these are

---

[1] Ruth Strang, *The Adolescent Views Himself, A Psychology of Adolescence* (New York: McGraw-Hill Book Company, 1957), p. 209.

translated into emotional states, which in turn, may be expressed in social behavior. Slow or rapid growth, unevenness of growth, or abnormalities of growth may affect an adolescent's total development.

In the succeeding sections of this study, an analysis of the various components of the socio-psychological development of transescents will be undertaken. It would be a serious error for any student of human growth to treat the physical, emotional, intellectual, and social aspects of development in an isolated manner. These facets do not evolve as separate entities. However, for the purposes of a detailed study, it is helpful to analyze such development first in a segmented manner and then from an interrelated standpoint.

Physical Growth

From a state of relative calm the transescent begins a period of accelerated development in late childhood. Most transescents have not had such a rapid growth spurt since infancy. They had been able to adjust rather well to the regular growth patterns of early and middle childhood. Gesell, Ilg, and Ames[2] point out that the child at this stage of development is the "picture of equipoise" and seems to be "a finished product of nature's handwork."

However, in the lives of most transescents, this fine state of physical adjustment is enjoyed only briefly. The onset of puberty brings an abrupt end to the stability prepubescents enjoyed. With it an upheaval in their life actions becomes commonplace and a period of adjustment to a chain of events begins, which will ultimately result in the child's becoming an adult.

The range of these growth changes is emphasized by Stolz and Stolz[3] in these remarks:

> Usually between the ages of eight years and twelve years among girls and between the nine years and thirteen years among boys there commences a sequence of changes in velocity of increase in height, body breadth and body depth, in heart size, lung capacity, muscular strength, and other structures and functions. This particular sequence of changes in the velocity of physical growth is unlike

---

[2] Arnold Gesell, Frances Ilg, and Louise Ames, *Youth, the Years from Ten to Sixteen* (New York: Harper & Row Publishers, 1956), p. 66.

[3] Herbert R. Stolz and Lois Meek Stolz, "Adolescent Problems Related to Somatic Variations" in *The Forty-third Yearbook of the National Society for the Study of Education, Part I Adolescence,* ed. Nelson B. Henry (Chicago: University of Chicago Press, 1944), p. 81.

anything which has occurred before and unlike anything which comes afterward. The sequence lasts for from four and one-half to seven and one-half years and is completed somewhere between the ages of fifteen and eighteen years in girls; between seventeen and twenty years in boys.

Of course, every transescent passes through a period characterized by these physical growth changes. If individual growth occurred simultaneously, according to a chronological age level, in all youngsters, there would not be as many social and emotional problems related to physical growth that now exists. Nature, however, follows no universal pattern with regard to group growth.

For the youngster variance in growth creates significant cause for concern. This is particularly true in the United States where cultural attitudes are so inextricably woven around physical appearance and strength. Movies, novels, television, and other media constantly stress the attributes of the beauty queen, such as "Miss Teen-Age America," for the girls, or, in the case of the boys, the "All-American" athlete.

Since these stereotypes represent the physically elite, it becomes even more difficult for transescents to associate their growth imperfections with this highly regarded example. Kuhlen[4] states in this respect, "Questions of normalcy of development are intensified by the social importance of developmental status." Stolz and Stolz[5] also use a cultural relationship as described in this passage:

> One boy seems to be unnecessarily worried because his shoulders are not broader, but it turns out that really he is disappointed in his whole pattern of physique. He would like to be (1) taller, (2) more broad shouldered, (3) bigger chested, (4) more heavily muscled; and it seems permissible to conclude that his problem of adjustment lies in the discrepancy between his inherited physique and the culturally suggested patterns of manhood which he has accepted.

Growth Trends

Another pertinent aspect of development is the timing of the onset of transescence. Presently, a marked trend in physical development is occurring. In this respect, Tanner[6] reports:

---

4 Raymond G. Kuhlen, *The Psychology of Adolescent Development* (New York: Harper & Row, Publishers, 1952), p. 73.

5 Stolz and Stolz, *op. cit.,* p. 91.

6 J. M. Tanner, *Growth at Adolescence* (Oxford: Blackwell Scientific Publications, 1962), pp. 143–144.

During the last 100 years there has been a very striking tendency for the time of adolescence, as typified by menarche or the growth spurt, to become earlier. The data on heights and weights of children of school age and before show that the whole process of growth has been progressively speeded up and that all age children born in the 1930s or 1950s, for example were considerably larger than those born in the 1900s. . . . The magnitude of the secular trend is very considerable and dwarfs the differences between socio-economic classes and between geographical regions within countries such as Sweden and the United States.

The trend in the United States is comparable to that reported throughout the Western world. Meredith[7] cites that in an age group from nine to fourteen years that, "Boys living in the United States today, white and Negro, are 6 to 8 percent taller and 12 to 15 percent heavier than was the case half a century ago." Mills[8] suggests a similar development in relating that this growth tide has resulted in a four-inch increase in stature in America and a steady year-by-year increase in height and weight among freshmen matriculating in American colleges. Espenschade and Meleney,[9] in a comparative study involving youngsters in the same school over a period from 1934–1935 to 1958–1959, found that girls in the later sample were one inch taller and six pounds heavier and that the boys in the more recent study were over two inches taller and ten pounds heavier. These researchers[10] also reported that the 1958–1959 youngsters were superior in the areas of jump and reach, the dynamometric strength pull test, and that today's boys excelled in throw for distance, the Brace test, and grip strength.

This growth acceleration has been accompanied by acceleration in other body areas. Simmons and Greulich[11] report that the average girl experiences her greatest height increment during the year preceding menarche; maximum increment does occur during the year

---

[7] Howard V. Meredith, "Stature and Weight of Children of the United States with Reference to the Influence of Racial, Regional, Socio-economic, and Secular Factors," *American Journal of Diseases of Childhood*, LXII (November, 1941), 932.

[8] C. A. Mills, "Temperature Influence Over Human Growth and Development," *Human Biology*, XXII (February, 1950), 71.

[9] Anna Espenschade and Helen E. Meleney, "Motor Performance of Boys and Girls," *The Research Quarterly of the American Association of Health, Physical Education and Recreation*, XXXII (May, 1961), 187.

[10] *Ibid.*, pp. 186–189.

[11] K. Simmons and W. W. Greulich, "Menarcheal Age and the Height, Weight and Skeletal Ages of Girls Age 7–17 Years," *Journal of Pediatrics*, XXII (May, 1943), 518.

of the menarche and some girls with late menarche seem to experience little or no premenarcheal acceleration.

Clements, Davies-Thomas, and Pickett[12] report a trend toward earlier eruption of teeth in the pubescent group and they indicate that if children are regularly examined in this period that the early eruption of the second molar may be associated with early puberty. This position was also taken by Boas[13] in an earlier study in which he cited the correlation between early increase in stature and early dentition. A similar occurrence is detectable in eye growth. Tanner[14] indicates that myopia is a frequent condition in pubescents and that myopia is occurring at an earlier age.

Sexual Development

Transescence is a period of physical change not only anatomically but also physiologically, as related to the reproductive system. Transescent sexual development appears to begin (in a rudimentary sense) a few years prior to the onset of puberty. Nathanson, Towne and Aub[15] indicate that between the ages of nine and twelve an increase in production of estrogens, the female hormone, occurs in the young girl. This marks the beginning of a long series of changes in the psychological and physical transformation of the girl into a woman. A small excretion of androgens, male hormones, occurs in the girl several years before the actual onset of puberty. In the case of the boys, the increase in male hormones is less accentuated than the increase in female estrogens and occurs over a greater time span.

The initial onset of puberty in boys is difficult to assess. Boys do not have an event, such as menstruation, to dramatically indicate pubescence. However, several characteristics may be considered: ejaculation, voice change, nocturnal emissions, and growth of pubic hair. Ramsey's[16] findings, based on 291 case histories obtained by personal interviews, indicate the following percentages in relation to

12 E. M. Clements, E. Davies-Thomas, and K. G. Pickett, "Time of Eruption of Permanent Teeth in Bristol Children in 1947–48," *British Medical Journal,* I (1953), 1423.

13 F. Boas, "Studies in Growth II," *Human Biology,* V (September, 1933), 444.

14 Tanner, *op. cit.,* p. 145.

15 I. T. Nathanson, L. Towne, and J. C. Aub, "Urinary Sex Hormone Studies," *Monographs of the Society for Research in Child Development,* VIII (1943), 70–81.

16 Glenn V. Ramsey, "The Sexual Development of Boys," *American Journal of Psychology,* LVI (1943), 217–233.

chronological age: at age ten, 1.8 percent had experienced ejaculation and by the end of age fourteen 87.3 percent had this experience. Voice change had occurred in 3 percent of the cases at age ten and 86.4 percent by the end of the fourteenth year. With regard to nocturnal emissions, 3 percent had this occurrence at age ten and by the end of the fourteenth year 39.6 percent had these emissions. Relative to the growth of pubic hair, 3 percent had begun this growth at age ten while almost all boys in this sample, 95.7 percent, had pubic hair by the end of age fourteen.

Transescent boys who have experienced ejaculation also have an increase in sexual interests and demands. Kuhlen[17] remarks:

> The age when sex interests and sex drives are aroused, and the possible relations of the arousal of sex drive and responsiveness to pubescence, are matters of interest. . . . Various studies show different results, but agreement exists that autoerotic practices begin in many cases before pubescence is reached.

The beginning of the menstrual cycle highlights the onset of puberty in the female transescent. The chronological age for the initiation of pubescence and menstruation has been the subject of much research. Jersild[18] indicates that the average girl reaches the menarche approximately at age thirteen but that this average is insignificant because there are such wide variations.

Earlier Sexual Maturation

Commensurate with the previously suggested reports of secular growth trends, a similar phenomenon exists in the earlier onset of menarche and sexual maturation. Tanner[19] describes this acceleration in these words:

> The acceleration of growth is also shown in the marked secular trend in age of menarche . . . the average ages at menarche from 1830 to 1960 in Norway, Sweden, Finland, Great Britain and Germany, together with data from entrants to a woman's college in the United States. . . . The trend is remarkably similar in all the series, and over the whole period plotted. Age at menarche has been getting earlier by some 4 months per decade in Western Europe

---

17 Kuhlen, *op. cit.*, p. 43.
18 Arthur T. Jersild, *The Psychology of Adolescence* (New York: The Macmillan Company, 1963), p. 12.
19 Tanner, *op. cit.*, p. 43.

over the period of 1830–1960. Other European data . . . and other American data, though not quite so regular, agree well with these figures. The trend in height and weight at about this age is closely equivalent to this amount of 4 months per decade, children of 10 thirty years ago having the size of children of 9 at present.

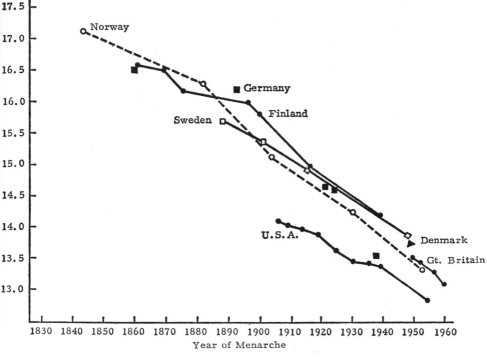

Figure 3. Age and Year Menarche.

An American study by Gould and Gould[20] confirms the earlier trend in menarche. These researchers discovered that daughters were menstruating .38 years sooner than their mothers.

Figure 3[21] indicates rather sharply this trend in menarche.

---

[20] H. N. Gould and M. R. Gould, "Age of First Menstruation in Mothers and Daughters," *Journal of the American Medical Association*, XCVIII (1932), 1349–1352.

[21] Tanner, *op. cit.*, p. 152.

Variables Affecting Maturation

It is helpful to investigate what the fundamental reasons are for secular trends in growth. Historically there seems to be evidence that trends in growth may be cyclic. Mills[22] reports on this historical aspect:

> There are several indications that human advance comes in long undulations of progress and recession, and that these waves are truly biologic. . . . In the time of ancient Greece there occurred a crest somewhat similar to the present. In stature and body build the ancient Greeks were the equal of, or perhaps superior to, present day people, and Hippocrates stated that the menses usually began at the age of 13. In philosophy and power of cerebration, in literature and art, in government, and in many other ways, evidence indicates an ancient Grecian crest in human development comparing very favorably with the most advanced groups of today. Through the intervening centuries of darkness and recession, however, man slumped in form and achievement. The giants and warriors of the Middle Ages were mere pigmies compared to present day military standards. . . . Body height of men during this period seems to have receded to about the level of prehistoric man (5 ft. 1 to 2 inches). Even early in the 19th century, the average male height in England was 3 inches less than it is today. Shortness of stature and slenderness of form were matched also by lateness in onset of puberty, records of over a century ago showing an onset of the menses usually in the 17th or 18th year.

Researchers have analyzed several variables which were considered partially responsible for earlier maturation. The relationship of growth to temperature and climate was studied by Mills[23] who found that a severe unseasonably warm period in the 1930's seemed to halt the growth tide, but he discovered in later research that this reversal, although definite, was only temporary. Whitacre and Grimes[24] compared the northern Texas cities of Lubbock and Denton with two southern Texas cities, San Antonio and Houston, to determine the effect of climate on growth. These cities have fairly different climatic conditions. Although a faster growth rate was discovered in

---

[22] C. A. Mills, "Geographic and Time Variations in Body and Age at Menarche," *Human Biology,* IX (February, 1937), 53–54.

[23] C. A. Mills, "Temperature Influence Over Human Growth and Development," *Human Biology,* XXII (February, 1950), 71–74.

[24] Jesse Whitacre and Ethel Grimes, "Some Body Measurements of Native Born White Children of Seven to Fourteen Years in Different Climatic Regions of Texas," *Child Development,* XXX (1959), 177–209.

the southern cities, the writers were inclined to believe that the differences could possibly be explained by other factors, such as bodily health, intellectual development, social adjustment, and economics as well as by climate. In a similar study related to climate, Wilson and Sutherland[25] stated:

> . . . that the menarche occurs relatively late in the hot dry climate of the Northern Nigerian savannah (14.4 years, with a remarkably low standard deviation), on the more temperate plateau (14.50 years), and in central India (14.65 years).

In this study, however, there was a difference between rural groups in Ceylon, who experienced onset at 14.39 years and urban children in Colombo whose onset was at 12.84 years. This range prompted these investigators[26] to state:

> The groups of children studied differ in food habits, nutritional status, and social environment as well as in climate and race. Without much more extensive observation it is not possible to assess the relative importance of these differences in influencing the age of menarche.

Racial factors may have a significant effect on secular growth, but due to their close association with socio-economic conditions, the true racial effect is quite difficult to assess. Ramsey[27] found no significant difference among 37 Negro boys and 286 white boys with reference to the median age of first ejaculation (13.8 years for both Negro and Caucasian), median age for appearance of pubic hair (13.3 years for the Negro and 13.6 for the Caucasian), and the median age for voice change (13.7 for the Negro and 13.4 for the Caucasian). Tanner[28] points out possible occurrences of racial and national differences in the growth rate in the following comments:

> Differences in growth-rate, both in size and proportions, certainly exist irrespective of environment between national or racial groups of different average physique. The rate of weight gain between age 6 and 8 is greater in children of American-born parents and ancestry than in American children of Italian parents, even within groups matched for socio-economic circumstances. . . . De-

---

[25] Dagmar Wilson and Ian Sutherland, "The Age of the Menarche in the Tropics," *British Medical Journal,* II (1953), 608.

[26] *Ibid.,* p. 608.

[27] Glenn V. Ramsey, "Sexual Growth of Negro and White Boys," *Human Biology,* XXII (May, 1950), 149.

[28] Tanner, *op. cit.,* p. 107.

spite being in worse economic and probably nutritional circumstances the American Indian children were at all ages heavier for
their height than the whites.

Nutrition has been found to be a highly influential variable in relation to the growth spurt. Since the world has undergone periods of
nutritional deficiency caused by various events such as famine, de-
pression, and war, this variable has been studied closely. Its effect
on adolescence has been one of retardation. Tanner[29] writes, "Adolescence under these circumstances simply waits until the body has
grown, however slowly, to approximate its normal adolescent size
or . . . maturity." In a study done in Stuttgart, Germany by Howe
and Schiller,[30] a unique opportunity presented itself, allowing for an
examination of the effect of nutrition on growth over a forty-year
time period, including two wars and several economic upturns and
recessions. These scientists summarized their findings as follows:

> Changes in food supply or the general availability of food and
> exposure to sunlight appear to be reflected by the growing child,
> particularly the rapidly growing adolescent child. A slowing down
> in rate of growth, both in height and weight, usually occurs when
> there is a marked reduction in the caloric protein, vitamin or min-
> eral content of the diet; conversely an accelerated rate of growth,
> up to the inherited capacity to grow, occurs with an adequate diet.

Generally, one postulates that the current trend toward earlier
physical maturation, barring catastrophic events, will continue.
There appears to be a very significant relationship between socio-
economic conditions and early growth. In the United States today,
socio-economic conditions seem favorable for a continuation of the
acceleration pattern. There are also indications that the range between socio-economic levels in America is narrowing. Gow, Holzner, and Pendleton[31] comment on this homogenization in these
words:

> Now even our so-called "hidden poverty," after too long neglect,
> has come under concerted attack by a society that realizes the pov-

---

[29] *Ibid.*, p. 123.

[30] Paul Howe and Marie Schiller, "Growth Responses of the School Child to
Change in Diet and Environmental Factors," *Journal of Applied Physiology,*
V (August, 1952), 51–61.

[31] J. Steele Gow, Jr., Burkart Holzner, and William C. Pendleton, "Economic,
Social, and Political Forces," *The Changing American School,* Sixty-fifth Year-
book of the National Society for the Study of Education, Part II, (Chicago, Ill.:
Distributed by the University of Chicago Press, 1966), p. 173.

erty cycle no longer need be tolerated as the inevitable lot of any of its people. On the whole, the general rise in the level of income has made income differentials within the vast middle range less noticeable than they used to be. The growth of an enormous mass market and new production technologies have brought former prestige items, such as the automobile and the family home, into the reach of a great many more families, so that social differentiation by consumption patterns while still obvious is far less pronounced than in the period before World War II, during which particularly in the large industrial centers, a huge working class lived in conspicuously different circumstances from the then much narrower middle and upper classes. . . .

Emotional and Social Implications of Maturation

To a large extent, transescent adjustment to the maturation process depends on what sort of relationship the youngster can achieve with both his adult and peer associates. Some transescents are able to adjust to growth changes because they understand or have been appropriately instructed in this area, or because their growth patterns conform to societal expectations. However, in other instances where atypical growth patterns, or a lack of personal security exists, transescents may undergo emotional stress affecting interpersonal relations.

Because of cultural expectations, the wide range of chronological ages during which puberty can occur tends to affect the child's life in an emotional manner. Physical development occurring at different ages may be either a source of anxiety or a source of accomplishment. This dual reaction tends to affect the transescent's security. Staton[32] comments on this condition:

> Often the girl has ambivalent feelings regarding her developing breasts, proud of her visible maturation and yet embarrassed and intensely self-conscious at the open display they make of her sex. . . . Much of the girl's self-consciousness, either pride or embarrassment, about her breast development is attributable to the influence of pictures on book covers, in movies, and movie ads, and in magazines which have in mid-century America made an erotic fetish of the breast, particularly the full, conspicuous breast.

In a similar way, the onset of menstruation often has a marked

---

[32] Thomas F. Staton, *Dynamics of Adolescent Adjustment* (New York: The Macmillan Company, 1963), p. 309.

effect on the transescent. Abel and Joffee[33] review a few of these possible reactions when they state:

> The emotional effects of the menarche on the American girl are dependent upon a large number of factors both psychological and cultural. Girls who are not informed in advance or ill-informed state that its appearance gave them a shock, particularly concerned that they had been injured in some way. Girls who for some reason feel guilty and insecure in relation to a parent or some other individual may associate the first menstruation with these feelings and believe that the blood has been sent as a punishment. On the other hand, girls . . . who have prior knowledge about the menarche feel pride at the onset of menstruation since it makes them "like their friends." One seventh grade group of girls formed a club to which each girl paid a quarter when her menarche appeared. All the class knew who was a "woman" and could belong to a club and who was still a "girl." But yet these girls also reported annoyance and anger at menstruation and a feeling of unfairness that boys were let off easy.

The reaction of girls who have not attained menarche also shows anxiety. This delay often prompts girls to wonder why nothing has occurred and leads them to think that perhaps they are not "normal."

Differentiation of growth and its relation to behavior has been the focal point of considerable research. Mussen and Jones[34] relate that early maturing boys present a much more favorable psychological picture than late maturing boys do. The latter will likely have negative self-conceptions, feelings of inadequacy, strong feelings of being rejected and dominated, prolonged dependency needs, and even rebellious attitudes toward their parents. In an extensive and valuable longitudinal study, Jones[35] reported through a comparative technique that (1) early maturing boys usually were leaders, while late maturers gave evidence of needing to counteract their physical disadvantage in some way, usually by striving for attention or withdrawal, and (2) that patterns exhibited by a group of late maturing boys at the age of seventeen years did not substantially alter by age

---

[33] Theodore M. Abel and Natalie F. Joffee, "Cultural Background of Female Puberty," *American Journal of Psychotherapy,* IV (January, 1950), 107.

[34] P. H. Mussen and M. C. Jones, "Self-Conceptions, Motivations, and Inter-Personal Attitudes of Late and Early Maturing Boys," *Child Development,* XXVIII (June, 1957), 255.

[35] M. C. Jones, "The Late Careers of Boys Who Were Early or Late Maturing Boys," *Child Development,* XXVIII (March, 1957), 113–128.

thirty-three. In the most recent statement coming out of this longi-tudinal study using the same sample (now age forty), Jones[36] relates:

> In general it has been shown that boys who are accelerated in physical development in adolescence seem to be advantaged in the peer culture. In adulthood, although physical differences no longer distinguish the extreme maturity groups, some psychological differ-ences still exist. The early developers cling to their early success pattern, continue to be well socialized to make a good impression. Late developers, carrying over a childhood pattern, are adventurous, rebellious, and assertive. They are also more flexible, a finding that suggests some possibly salutory effects of what was interpreted as an adolescent social disadvantage.

With similar results, Shonfeld[37] examined 256 late maturing boys ages 9 to 16 who presented personality and emotional difficulties stemming from fears of physical inadequacy. He concluded that a delay in age for the onset of sexual maturation, the failure of the growth spurt to begin, or any inadequacy of masculine development could lead to a variety of personality and psychosomatic complaints being made in the early part of the second decade of life.

A comparable pattern of behavior is observed in female transes-cents. Early maturers generally have a much better reaction in their relations with others than do retarded maturers. More[38] indicates that early maturing girls are more independent, have less conflicts with inner values, have fewer feelings of inner guilt, and are more realistic in their self-evaluations than late maturers—who tend to believe they are unloved, misunderstood, and uncared for. In a study by Stolz and Stolz,[39] it was disclosed that 41 percent of the adolescent girls participating in the University of California's Insti-tute of Child Welfare studies suffered known anxieties concerning physical factors.

Differences among girls of the same age, who have and who have

---

36 Mary C. Jones, "Psychological Correlates of Somatic Development," *News-letter, Division of Developmental Psychology of the American Psychological As-sociation* (Fall, 1964), p. 2.

37 W. A. Shonfeld, "Inadequate Masculine Physique as a Factor in Personality Development of Adolescent Boys," *Psychosomatic Medicine,* XII (1950), 53.

38 Douglas M. More, "Developmental Concordance and Discordance During Puberty and Early Adolescence," *Monographs of the Society for Child Develop-ment, Inc.,* XVIII (1953), 35–36.

39 Stolz and Stolz, *op. cit.,* p. 86.

not experienced the onset of menstruation, offer basis for analysis. Stone and Barker[40] discovered differences in interest patterns. They report that a greater proportion of post menarchial girls than pre-menarchial girls (of the same chronological age) have a greater interest in personal adornment, are less interested in vigorous physical activities, but more interested in daydreaming activities. In a related study in Grades 6 through 9, Faust[41] studied physical maturity in order to ascertain if maturity in transescent girls determines prestige. She[42] found that prestige was enhanced in Grades 7, 8, and 9 if menstruation had occurred relatively early. However, early development tended to be a detriment to prestige among sixth grade girls.

Social relations of male transescents reflects that a similarly favorable position in males results from sexual maturity. Indicative of this reaction are the results of a study by Latham[43] who reported that, in junior high school, boys who possessed more sexual maturity tended to be viewed by their peers as athletic leaders. Jones and Bayley[44] registered similar results. They rated early maturing boys as being more relaxed, more attractive physically, more assured, more grown-up, and more likely to have older friends than late maturing boys.

One concludes from these research findings that it is the early maturer who is less likely to have social-emotional problems in our society. Conversely, the probability is high that the late maturer will be emotionally disadvantaged in an educational setting—particularly if that setting compounds tensions. Angelo, Dollins, and Mech[45] comment on this condition:

> Certainly it is almost axiomatic to state that a child cannot be expected to do good school work, particularly in such problem solving

[40] C. P. Stone and R. G. Barker, "The Attitudes and Interests of Premenarcheal and Postmenarcheal Girls," *Journal of Genetic Psychology,* LIV (1939), 61–62.

[41] M. S. Faust, "Developmental Maturity as a Determinant in Prestige of Adolescent Girls," *Child Development,* XXXI (1960), 182–183.

[42] *Ibid.*

[43] A. J. Latham, "The Relationship Between Pubertal Status and Leadership to Junior High School Boys," *Journal of Genetic Psychology,* LXXVIII (1951), 185–194.

[44] M. C. Jones and N. Bayley, "Physical Maturing Among Boys as Related to Behavior," *Journal of Educational Psychology,* XLI (1950), 129–148.

[45] Henry Angelo, Joseph Dollins, and Edmond Mech, "Trends in the Fears and Worries of School Children as Related to Socio-Economic Status and Age," *Journal of Genetic Psychology,* LXXXIX (1956), 263.

activities as are required in academic skills, if he or she is emotionally disturbed, anxious, or worried. No human organism can perform at maximum efficiency under such a burden.

Other authors believe that for transescents school emphasis should center on areas related to social-emotional areas. Havighurst[46] succinctly points out, "The period from twelve to eighteen is primarily one of physical and emotional maturing. . . . The principal lessons are emotional and social, not intellectual."

Frank, *et al.,*[47] emphasize this contention by relating the following sentiments:

> The schools often make demands for sustained study and academic achievement and expect students to be actively interested in various subject matters and intellectual skills at a time just before and after puberty when most girls are least capable of meeting those demands and sustaining such interest except by sacrifice of what is of crucial importance to their maturation and at a psychological cost which may be excessive.

Physical Efficiency

In the life of the transescent, one discovers that not only the appearance of the body is of concern, but the efficiency of its use is important. Due to the nature of the American culture, physical efficiency is decidedly more important in the life of the boy than it is for the girl. The American boy is expected to be the rugged, manly stereotype. Toby[48] states:

> Although male infants cry just as much as female infants when they are hurt, American society teaches older boys to respond to pain differently from girls. The same level of physical suffering that causes American women to cry produces curses from American men or silent heroism.

The girl, on the other hand, gains greatest status from an attractive appearance. In transescence, while a boy gains prestige to the degree he can successfully participate in physical activities, the girl

---

[46] Robert J. Havighurst, *Developmental Tasks and Education* (New York: David McKay Company, Inc., 1952), p. 33.

[47] L. K. Frank, R. Harrison, E. Hellersberg, K. Machover, and M. Steiner, "Personality Development in Adolescent Girls," *Monographs of the Society for Research in Child Development, Inc.,* XVI (1951), pp. 205–206.

[48] Jackson Toby, *Contemporary Society* (New York: John Wiley and Sons, Inc., 1964), p. 4.

often experiences social problems if she is physically proficient. Horrocks[49] comments on the effect of physical efficiency on boys:

> If the young boy lacks any of these attributes, he must seek other means of finding social approval and acceptance, but no matter what these other means may be he is always exposed to criticism or even contempt when he comes into contact with those who are athletically more successful. This does not mean that a boy must be a stellar athlete to find acceptance. He may deviate considerably, as most boys do, from a norm of great physical prowess, but his deviation may go only so far; physical activity and interest must appear to at least some degree in his activities.

For a boy social approval through athletics incurs not only pressure from his peers (which is of great importance) but also from adults. Unfortunately, our culture makes this demand at an inopportune period as far as the transescent's physical maturation is concerned. Reichert[50] amplifies this contention by maintaining that preadolescent and adolescent children are at a physically disadvantaged age relative to athletics. Bone growth is occurring at a more rapid rate than is muscular development. This results in a lack of protection for the bones by the covering muscles and supporting tendons. Reichert[51] further suggests that strenuous athletics can tend to alter bone position, causing added stress and even possible physical damage.

Here, as in so many instances, the transescent is enveloped in a dilemma caused by the expectations of an external force, which he may or may not be able to meet, depending upon his personal capabilities.

Implications for Education

The preceding section contains two significant and interrelated points. The first being that human growth patterns are undergoing subtle constant alteration in the direction of earlier maturation. The preponderance of research clearly indicates that, physically, with each passing decade youngsters are beginning their ascent to adulthood sooner. This earlier maturation pattern is augmented by a

---

49 J. E. Horrocks, *The Psychology of Adolescence* (Boston: Houghton Mifflin Company, 1962), pp. 414–415.

50 J. L. Reichert, "Competitive Athletics for Pre-Teen Age Children," *Journal of the American Medical Association,* CLXVI (1958), 1701–1707.

51 *Ibid.*

favorable socio-economic state, and there is every indication that this phenomenon will continue. Secondly, in our culture, the onset of transescence creates many internal and external pressures for children over which they have little control. This often results in emotional and social anxiety and tension. The adjustment made by transescents to their environment depends largely on growth patterns in relation to cultural expectations.

A careful analysis of the nature of transescent physical growth suggests that there are several primary implications for the educator. Foremost is the realization that the focal point for the learning process is the child's growth needs. This statement seems almost axiomatic, and yet, oftentimes, the nature of the child plays a secondary role. Prescott[52] indicates this by remarking, "Currently, many school people seem to feel that the child is a mechanism and that learning occurs in a child chiefly as a result of something that is done to him from the outside." The point is all too clear that educators have a responsibility to consider the transescent's needs as the "engine" and not the "caboose" of the educational "train."

This position infers that school programs should be founded on goals which will enable the physically emerging youth to better understand growth changes in order to keep a proper perspective; to create goals which will enable all boys, not just the physically gifted, to attain physical success; and to develop goals which will aid girls in understanding the reasons for the presence or absence of maturation changes.

Armed with knowledge about the physical nature of the transescent, educators must have conviction and courage to initiate and to maintain educational processes compatible with this knowledge.

---

[52] Daniel A. Prescott, *Factors That Influence Learning, Horace Mann Lecture, 1958* (Pittsburgh: University of Pittsburgh, 1958), p. 7.

CHAPTER III

Mental Growth

In the preceding chapter, an analysis of patterns of physical growth was undertaken in an effort to ascertain the implications on transescent growth. This chapter will study intellectual growth similarly.

Intellectual processes have significant implications for the educator of transescents. A curricular program has little chance for success if it is incompatible with the nature of the students which it is attempting to educate. There is a need for the transescent educator to be aware of the effect of cultural variables on the development of the intellect, since the degree of intellectual attainment appears to be enhanced or retarded thereby.

Intellectual Nature of Transescence

Intellectual growth appears to follow a course marked by sequential stages, in which the learner is capable of interacting with the environment in a manner commensurate with his level of development. This does not infer that all people eventually will attain the same stage level of development or that all transescents are at the same stage of development by virtue of a similarity of chronological age. What it does contend is that the various stages of development occur in a similar sequence for learners and that these stages are identifiable.

One of the primary goals in the construction of a transescent socio-psychological model is the determination of intellectual characteristics. In this respect, there seems considerable merit in consulting the work of Jean Piaget. He and his colleagues have collected, by means of clinical research, a wealth of data regarding the intellectual characteristics of the learner at various stages of development. Although the philosophy and history of Piaget's work is of distinct importance, the facet of his endeavors, which is most pertinent for an educational model, is his description of the learner at transescence.

This Geneva group study segmented intellectual growth into three stages. They label these levels: (1) preoperations, (2) concrete operations, and (3) formal operations. These broad stages are further refined into sub-stages. It appears from their analysis that the relevant stages for transescents are the levels of concrete operations and formal operations. In various transescent schools, the preponderance of youngsters may be in one or the other stage, depending on various factors to be discussed later. This does not alter the suggestion that a transescent educator will likely be constructing educational processes based both on the stages of concrete operations and formal operations. Any brief summary of Piaget's massive contribution involves the risk of overgeneralization. Despite this obvious danger, the most relevant facets invite analysis.

Although emphasis will be placed on later stages of mental development, the level of preoperations requires some explanation as a background for later developments. In this stage, children from birth to approximately school age gradually acquire an awareness of the external world. Their interaction with the environment is of a trial and error nature, with success or failure being of prime importance. Throughout their actions, preoperational youngsters find it very difficult to separate themselves from the object of their actions. Thus, in general, the preoperational child is involved primarily with his own goals.

One ability, which is very much a part of later development, is missing. This ability, to which Piaget refers, is the property of reversibility. If an object changes shape, the first stage youngster cannot mentally reverse the procedure. An illustration of this lack of mental reversibility is in the following Piagetian experiment: the experimenter has two round balls of clay. He changes one ball of clay into a different shape. At this stage the child will not be able to mentally reverse the new shape back to its original form, and will believe that the mass is not the same.

Upon attainment of the first stage, the child begins the concrete operations phase of development. Educationally, this level begins approximately as the child enters school and usually extends through the upper elementary years. At this point, the child's processes tend to become more internalized as compared to the external trial and error process of the earlier stage. Now the child is able not only to get information to the mind but is capable of using this information in an organized way in solving problems. The youngster now sorts out possibilities for solutions by using acquired information as opposed to his former activity of engaging in trial and error solutions. As this stage evolves toward culmination, children develop cognitive ability to a high degree.

Flavell[1] underscores Piaget's basic tenet surrounding the concrete operations stage:

> . . . if we look with a Piagetian eye, we see one higher order difference which subsumes all the particulars; and from this one difference stems most of what Piaget has to say about the sub-period of concrete operations. It is simply that the older child seems to have at his command a coherent and integrative cognitive system with which he organizes and manipulates the world around him. Much more than his younger counterpart, he gives the decided impression of possessing a solid cognitive bedrock, something flexible and plastic and yet consistent and enduring with which he can structure the present in terms of the past without undue strain and dislocation; that is, without the ever present tendency to tumble into the perplexity and contradiction which mark the preschooler . . . most of what Piaget's detailed account of concrete operations is an elaboration of this fundamental point.

What are a few of the characteristics of this "solid cognitive bedrock"? One feature is the ability to reverse one's thinking, or in effect, not only to proceed from start to finish in a mental sequence, but also the ability to return to the starting phase of the sequence or to any point in the sequence. Thus, a youngster cannot only multiply 4 x 4 and get 16, but he can also reverse the procedure to discover that the square root of 16 is 4. The concrete operational child sees both a direct and an inverse relationship when attempting to place objects or symbols serially. Piaget's work is steeped in mathematics and science; nevertheless, this same principle can be applied to other areas of the curriculum. An illustration in history: the ability to see not only the chain of events leading to the outbreak of a conflict, but also to see how changing one of the events in a sequence might have restored the status quo rather than causing the conflict.

A second characteristic of concrete operations shows that at this stage the child is able to apply logic at a level not possible in the

---

[1] John Flavell, *The Developmental Psychology of Jean Piaget* (New York: D. Van Nostrand Company, Inc., 1963), p. 165.

preschooler. For example, in a series of three objects, A, B, and C, which have ascending weights, the child who possesses concrete operational ability would recognize that object B must be larger than A but smaller than C if it is to occupy a central position according to weight. In an experiment relating to equilibrium and balance, Inhelder and Piaget[2] illustrate this advance in logical reasoning by describing its results:

> At the earlier stage, when the subject comes across two weights which do not come into equilibrium, he works mostly with substitutions—addition or subtractions. In this way, he achieves certain equalization by displacement, but only exceptionally and by groping about (regulations). On the other hand, at the present stage the subject who comes to two unequal weights tries to balance them by means of an oriental displacement on the hypothesis that the same object "will weigh more" at a greater distance from the axis and less when brought closer to it.

This level of logical development seems applicable to the range of curricular areas. It is reasonable to expect a concrete operational child to apply the same logical approach to the principles of land irrigation, for example.

A child has made an important advance in the concrete operation stage when he can reason that two objects may possess similar properties regardless of their appearance. The Geneva group classifies this ability as conservation and have discovered that mental conservation of mass is detectable in youngster's thought in the early phases of concrete operations, while the ability to understand conservation of weight occurs in the later phases of the stage.

The concrete operations stage is quite impressive when compared to the preoperations stage. But it has, in the opinion of the Geneva group, definite limitations. These limitations appear to revolve around a child's initial approach to cognitive activity. Flavell[3] effectively describes this difference in the following passage:

> But the starting point for concrete operations, as for preoperations, is always the real rather than the potential. The child of 7–11 years acts as though his primary task were to organize and order what is immediately present; the limited extrapolation of this organizing and ordering to the not-there is something he will do where

---

[2] Barbel Inhelder and Jean Piaget, *The Growth of Logical Thinking from Childhood to Adolescence* (New York: Basic Books, Inc., 1958), pp. 171–172.

[3] Flavell, *op. cit.,* pp. 203–204.

necessary, but this extrapolation is seen as a special case activity.
What he does not do (and what the adolescent does do) is delineate
all possible eventualities at the outset and then try to discover which
of these possibilities really do occur in the present data; in this latter
strategy, the real becomes a special case of the possible, not the
other way around.

The third and final stage of intellectual development, according
to the Geneva group, is the formal operations stage. This level occurs after the attainment of concrete operations and usually comes
into existence during the period of transescence. At this stage, most
youngsters develop the ability to think logically, in the manner of
the scientist. Bruner[4] depicts this stage as follows:

> After two decades of research, Piaget and his associates have
> traced the development of thinking to the stage where contemporary
> western man reaches his full logical powers. These powers rest in
> man's capacity after a long period of biological and cultural prepa-
> rations, to carry out intellectual operations that appear to be based
> in the implicit structure of formal logic. Somewhere between 12 and
> 14 years of age, with the development of ability to reflect upon
> thought itself, the adolescent begins to show the marks of formal
> thinking. He is now ready to take his place as a scientist, a thinker,
> a spinner of theory.

Since the majority of transescents enter this level during their stay
in the middle school, it is important to analyze some of the basic
intellectual characteristics of formal operations. The keystone of this
stage is the reversal of mental operations. It has been emphasized
that, prior to formal operations, the child always started with the
real and moved toward the potential. As he progressed, the youngster began envisaging a whole host of possibilities and, through
reasoning and experimentation, deduced answers.

A second characteristic of formal operations is cited by Flavell[5]
as propositional thinking. The youngster at this stage takes the results of concrete operations and formulates propositions which then
are exploited further in an effort to make various kinds of logical
connections between them. In effect, the youngster capitalizes on
previously formed cognitive processes.

A third characteristic of this stage, reported by Flavell,[6] is the

---

4 J. S. Bruner, "Inhelder and Piaget's *The Growth of Logical Thinking,* A Psychologist's Viewpoint," *British Journal of Psychology,* L (1959), 363.

5 Flavell, *op. cit.,* p. 205.

6 *Ibid.,* p. 206.

capacity for combinatorial analysis. The formal operations thinker not only isolates all possible variables, but also sees them in their fullest range of combinations.

This type of reasoning has many curricular implications. At this level, the transescent is capable not only of learning that Columbus sailed in 1492, but infinitely more challenging, the entire range of complex causal factors involved in the voyage is available for mental interpretation.

Flavell[7] ties together the processes of formal operations in the following paradigm:

> He begins by organizing the various elements of the data with the concrete-operational techniques of middle childhood. These organized elements are then cast in the form of statements or propositions which can be combined in various ways. Through the method of combinatorial analysis he then isolates for consideration the totality of distinct combinations of these propositions. These combinations are regarded as hypotheses, some of which will be confirmed and some infirmed by subsequent investigation. . . . The adolescent views his task as that of determining the actual shape of things by successively putting them to empirical test.

Characteristics of Stage Development

In the preceding discussion, various intellectual stage characteristics were cited. For the educator not only a knowledge of these traits is of value, but knowing the manner in which they evolve is significant. The subsequent discussion will analyze this evolutionary process of mental growth.

A succinct statement relative to stage development is given by Inhelder[8] who summarizes the criteria of stage development in these words:

> Like many other authors, Piaget describes cognitive development in terms of stages. Whereas somatic and perceptual development seems to be continuous, intellectual development seems to take place in stages, the criteria of which can be defined as follows:
> 1. Each stage involves a period of formation (Genesis) and a period of attainment. Attainment is characterized by the

---

[7] *Ibid.*

[8] Barbel Inhelder, "Some Aspects of Piaget's Genetic Approach to Cognition," *Monographs of the Society for Research in Child Development: Thought in the Young Child,* XXVII (1962), 23.

progressive organization of a composite structure of mental operation.

2. Each structure constitutes at the same time the attainment of one stage and the starting point of the next stage, of a new evolutionary process.
3. The order of succession of the stages is constant. Ages of attainment can vary within certain limits as a function of factors of motivation, exercise, cultural milieu, and so forth.
4. The transition from an earlier to a later stage follows a law of implication analogous to the process of integration, preceding structures becoming a part of later structures.

Inhelder's summation raises certain questions. How does one develop intellectually? By what processes do cognitive manifestations occur enabling one to evolve more and more complex abilities?

Again, it seems valid to turn to the work of Piaget and his introspective interpreter, Flavell, for at least a rudimentary orientation regarding the acquisition of cognitive structures. Permeating Piaget's outlook is a consistent biological thread. Flavell[9] states, "For Piaget, the one-time biologist, intelligence can be meaningfully considered only as an extension of certain biological characteristics, fundamental in the sense that they obtain wherever life obtains."

Flavell[10] continues to expand this connection by stating:

> The positive, constructive something we inherit, Piaget argues, is a mode of intellectual functioning. We do not inherit cognitive structures as such; these come into being only in the course of development. What we do inherit is a *modus operandi,* a specific manner in which we transact business with the environment. There are two important general characteristics of this mode of functioning. First, it generates cognitive structures. Structures come into being in the course of intellectual functioning; it is through functioning, and only through functioning, that cognitive structures get formed. Second, and this is a most important point, the mode of functioning which Piaget says constitutes our biological heritage remains essentially constant throughout life. . . . It is because of this constancy of functioning in the face of changing structures that its fundamental properties . . . are referred to as functional invariants.

This passage seems to explain why at each stage a child seems to follow a similar path from genesis to attainment. It also implies why some youngsters pass through the various stages either earlier or later

---

[9] Flavell, *op. cit.,* pp. 41–42.
[10] *Ibid.,* p. 43.

than their peers. Thirdly, the preceding comments ferret out reasons why, with each succeeding stage attainment, individuals are able to scale greater cognitive heights.

Piaget believes, at all ages, there are basic vehicles or functional invariants through which mental growth takes place. One functional invariant, organization, permits mental operations to take place in a systematic manner. Flavell,[11] commenting on the organizational concept, says:

> An act of intelligence, be it a crude motor movement in infancy or a complex and abstract judgment in adulthood, is always related to a system of totality . . . the ontogenetic development of structures can be thought of as a process of successive approximations to a kind of ideal equilibrium, an end state never achieved.

It is helpful to assess the functional invariant which acts in the formulation of organizational structures. This invariant, Piaget asserts, is adaptation. It likewise has roots in a biological framework. Adaptation is made possible by the cognitive interaction of assimilation and accommodation, not unlike the physiological process the body encounters in the assimilation of food and the accommodation of the systems of the body to the assimilated nutrient. Continuing the biological analogy, the body is able to create structures based on this physiological adaptation process. Flavell[12] masterfully depicts the intellectual involvement of these Piagetian invariants in this way:

> Assimilation here refers to the fact that every cognitive encounter with an environmental object necessarily involves some kind of cognitive structuring (or restructuring) of that object in accord with the nature of the organisms existing intellectual organization. . . . Every act of intelligence, however, rudimentary and concrete, presupposes an interpretation of something in external reality, that is an assimilation of that something to some kind of meaning system in the subject's cognitive organization. . . . If intellectual adaptation is always and essentially an assimilatory act, it is no less an accommodatory one. . . . The essence of accommodation is precisely this process of adapting oneself to the variegated requirements or demands which the world of objects imposes upon one.

In the stage development concept, the organization-adaptation relationship must be sequential, that is, from a lower stage to a higher stage. This point is of interest because educators have shown

---

[11] *Ibid.*, p. 47.
[12] *Ibid.*, p. 48.

a desire to accelerate learning by placing advanced academic subjects which traditionally have been thought to be high school courses
in the junior high school. A caution regarding this procedure is im-
plied in Piaget's philosophy. Flavell[13] suggests in this respect:

> ... the organism can assimilate only those things which past assim-
> ilations have prepared it to assimilate. There must already be a
> system of meanings, an existing organization, sufficiently advanced
> that it can be modified to admit the candidates for assimilation
> which accommodation places before it. There can never be a radical
> rupture between the new and the old; events whose interpretation
> requires a complete extension or reorganization of the existing
> structure simply cannot be accommodated to and thence assimilated.

Thus, this position places considerable stress on the importance of
cognitive maturation.

Variables Affecting Intellectual Growth

The previous discussion emphasized the conditions necessary for
cognitive maturation. It is evident that there are variables acting to
reduce or to accelerate stage development. Certainly, there are sufficiently cogent reasons for a critical analysis of this premise.

The effect of experience plays an important role in the Piagetian
theory. Inhelder and Piaget[14] comment on this role with regard to
formal operations in this way:

> ... the age of 11–12 years may be, beyond neurological factors, a
> product of progressive acceleration of individual development under
> the influence of education, and perhaps nothing stands in the way of
> a further reduction of the average age in a more or less distant
> future. . . . A particular social environment remains indispensable
> for the realization of these possibilities. It follows that their realiza-
> tion can be accelerated or retarded as a function of cultural and
> educational conditions.

In American culture, experiences are interrelated with socio-
economic class. Davis[15] points out that parents in different social
classes instruct their youngsters differently. He states, "Class training

---

13 *Ibid.,* p. 50.

14 Barbel Inhelder and Jean Piaget, *The Growth of Logical Thinking from Childhood to Adolescence, loc. cit.,* p. 337.

15 Allison Davis, "Child Training and Social Class," *Child Behavior and Development,* ed. R. G. Barker, J. S. Koumin, and H. F. Wright (New York: Mc-
Graw-Hill Book Company, 1943), p. 609.

of the child ranges all the way from the control of the manner and ritual by which he eats his food to the control of his choice of playmates and of his educational and occupational goals." Havighurst[16] concurs by commenting on a very distressing aspect of this situation. He writes:

> It seems probable that our society actually discovers and develops no more than perhaps half its potential intellectual talent. Some evidence for this statement lies in the fact that former immigrant groups, which at one time did the heavy labor of America, at first produced very few mentally superior children; but after a sojourn in this country of two or three generations, they have produced large numbers of mentally superior children. They did this through bettering the environment in which they reared their children. The same process is now going on in the underprivileged groups of today —the Negroes, the Puerto Ricans, the rural southern whites—as they secure better economic conditions and then create a more favorable environment for their children.

Obviously, in these situations producing cultural deprivation, society must do everything possible to provide experiences to aid learning. There is a great deal of evidence to show, hopefully, that an attack on poverty is going to be a high priority goal in the ensuing years.

Experience in Piagetian doctrine does not appear to be a variable isolated from the central biological framework. It varies with the empirical view which, in part, states that experience is applied to the organism without much subject organization being necessary. Flavell[17] describes Piaget's position on this point by relating:

> Experience is therefore not a simple and indivisible entity, homogenous at every point in development in its insistent pressure upon the subject. But what can this fact mean, Piaget argues, but that it is the nature of the subject's activity which will determine how and to what extent experiences undergone will be used to modify future behavior.

Unlike many contemporary psychological thinkers, Piaget's concept of motivation is inextricably woven in the internal organiza-

---

[16] Robert J. Havighurst, "Conditions Productive of Superior Children," *Teachers College Record*, LXII (1961), 524–531. Reprinted by permission of author and publisher.
[17] Flavell, *op. cit.*, p. 69.

tion-adaptation biological process. Flavell[18] contrasts Piaget's belief with others in this way:

> What prompts the subject—infant, child or adult—to engage in cognitive activities *vis-a-vis* the environment? Perhaps the most common answer among psychologists at large is that these actions are motivated by primary drives—hunger, thirst, sex, etc.—or by secondary needs derived from these. Piaget does not deny the role of bodily needs and their derivatives but maintains that the fundamental motive governing intellectual endeavor is of a different sort entirely. His position is simply that there is an intrinsic need for cognitive organs or structures once generated by functioning, to perpetuate themselves by more functioning.

Piaget's learning theory emphasizes activity, curiosity, flexibility, exploration, and other related areas as substrates of the educational process.

Bayley[19] concisely summarizes the effect of the variables discussed in preceding paragraphs with these remarks:

> It becomes evident that the intellectual growth of any given child is a resultant of varied and complex factors. These will include his inherent capacities for growth, both in amount and in note of progress. They will include the emotional climate in which he grows; whether he is encouraged or discouraged, whether his drive (or ego involvement) is strong in intellectual thought processes or is directed to other aspects of his life field. And they will include the material environment in which he grows; the opportunities for experience and for learning, and the extent to which these opportunities are continuously geared to his capacity to respond and to make use of them. Evidently all of these things are influential in varying amounts for different individuals and for different stages in their growth.

Cultural factors not only affect rate of intellectual maturation, by virtue of a direct environmental relationship, but the indirect societal forces also are involved. The relationship of these forces with the transescent will be investigated in greater detail in the following chapter; however, their subtle impact on transescent intellectual growth bears a relevant consideration.

The demand for consistency again invites investigation of the stage development theorist's point of view. It is recalled that the

---

18 *Ibid.*, p. 78.
19 Nancy Bayley, "On the Growth of Intelligence," *American Psychologist,* X (1955), 813–814.

basic characteristic of formal operations is the child's ability to think largely in terms of the potential. This ability—to go beyond the concrete realities of the present—is closely allied with transescent effective behavior. Inhelder and Piaget[20] cite in this connection:

> Formal thinking is both thinking about thought . . . and a reversal of relations between what is real and what is possible. . . . These are two characteristics . . . which are the source of the living responses, always so full of emotion, which the adolescent uses to build his ideals in adapting to society. The adolescent's theory construction shows both that he has become capable of reflective thinking and that his thought makes it possible for him to escape the concrete present toward the realm of the abstract and the possible. . . . Once more logic is not isolated from life; it is no more than the expression of operational coordination essential to action.

An interesting point in this regard was disclosed by Jersild and Tasch.[21] In a study of children's interests they reported that:

> As the children grow older there is, in addition to the increase in wishes pertaining to other specific purposes, an increase also in wishes for benefits to mankind at large. Less than 3 percent of the children in the primary grades expressed wishes for the welfare of mankind as compared with about 12 percent of the children at the senior high school level.

It is reasonable to assume that the vast array of tension created by events occurring in the international and national scenes will have some impact on the effective behavior of transescents; however, these forces have an even more subtle effect on educators. The consequences for schools are great. DeYoung and Wynn[22] describe these pressures in the following passage:

> When Russia preceded the United States in placing a satellite in outer space, many people were sure that the sole fault lay with our schools. . . . When the number of cases of juvenile delinquency rises, there are those who see the cause clearly in the schools. If young people appear irreligious, it is concluded that the schools must be godless. If a soldier defects to the communists, the schools have failed to teach patriotism. Folks like to see simple answers for com-

---

[20] Inhelder and Piaget, *op. cit.*, pp. 341–342.

[21] Arthur T. Jersild and Ruth J. Tasch, *Children's Interests and What They Suggest for Education* (New York: Bureau of Publications, Teachers College, Columbia University, 1949), pp. 18–19.

[22] Chris DeYoung and Richard Wynn, *American Education* (New York: McGraw-Hill Book Company, 1964), p. 458.

plex problems. . . . Schools often mirror the values and shortcomings of society.

Naturally, educators are sensitive to criticism yet they must be responsible for supplying the impetus for change. Deviations from former patterns may be favorable or unfavorable to the learning process. For example, the widespread concern among educators and laymen over situations cited by DeYoung and Wynn has brought about some beneficial results: (1) curriculum analysis, (2) increased financial support for schools, and (3) a greater public awareness of the vital significance of education. Conversely, increased pressure for academic excellence has generated a demand for learning acceleration, exemplified by the current trend to uproot high school subjects and move them intact to lower grades. In itself, this is not necessarily harmful. But what seems to have happened is that a total movement of thought processes (involved in these subjects) has taken place without enough consideration being given to the mental characteristics of the younger students and the adjustments that they will have to make. The resultant emotional anxieties made possible through such indiscriminate curricular change may be a causal factor in the growing rate of students' emotional, physical, and academic difficulties.

As previously discussed, transescents undergo a period of physical instability and rapid change. Intellectual change, from concrete operations to formal operations, involves a far less radical departure from security than physical changes present. Nevertheless, Piaget's concept of egocentrism does involve a period of intellectual disequilibrium and it seems pertinent to discuss it here. Flavell[23] describes the processes involved in egocentrism in this way:

> In Piaget's theory, egocentrism is likely to increase whenever, as development proceeds, the child begins to cope with a new and untried field of cognitive action; i.e., whenever he enters a new plane of cognitive functioning. The burst of egocentrism slowly subsides as the child progressively masters the new field, only to reassert itself when still another new domain is approached. The ebb and flow of egocentrism across ontogenetic development is, of course, an expression—almost a simplified restatement—of the general equilibration model which Piaget imputes to cognitive evolution, that is, development as a series of successive disequilibrium → equilibrium subdevelopments.

---

[23] Flavell, *op. cit.*, p. 224.

The Geneva group's theory provides evidence that the medium through which egocentrism recedes is the social interaction of the formal thinker with his peers. Flavell[24] explains:

> . . . social interaction is the principal liberating factor, particularly social interaction with peers. In the course of his contacts (and especially, his conflicts and arguments) with other children, the child increasingly finds himself forced to reexamine his own precepts and concepts in the light of those of others, and by so doing, gradually rid himself of cognitive egocentrism.

If the curriculum is founded on an awareness of the nature of changing patterns of intellectual growth and their various needs, a favorable learning environment is obtained. However, a failure to recognize these changes will more than likely result in emotional stress. The role of emotions, relative to learning, is a vital one, as Prescott[25] indicates:

> Research has shown that minor frustrations and threats enliven the individual to greater effort and to reasonable risk taken for the sake of satisfying a need or realizing a goal. Mild emotions are tonic to both physical and mental processes and so have their constructive place at school.
>
> But frequent recurring or long-continued strong unpleasant emotions are another story. They produce anxiety, fear, and hostility and narrow the perception-readiness of the individual to matters relating to the need or frustration. The tendency of strong emotions to limit and reduce usual school learnings is clear.

The challenge to the transescent educator for creating an environment which will aid in the reduction of emotional tension is a crucial one. Certainly educational statesmanship demands that the learning environment be structured on the knowledge of intellectual characteristics, rather than being set up as a defense to current popular pressure.

Implications for Education

The development of intelligence is a vital national concern. Guilford[26] stresses this point when he comments:

---

[24] *Ibid.,* p. 279.

[25] Daniel A. Prescott, *Factors That Influence Learning* (Pittsburgh: University of Pittsburgh Press, 1958), pp. 48–49.

[26] J. P. Guilford, "Three Faces of Intellect," *American Psychologist,* XIV (1959), 469.

Two related events of very recent history make it imperative that we learn all we can regarding the nature of intelligence. I am referring to the advent of the artificial satellites and planets and to the crisis in education that has arisen in part as a consequence. The preservation of our way of life and our future security depend upon our most important natural resources.

These points to which Guilford alludes have profound implications for a transescent educational model. There is little doubt but that there is an urgency and a need for developing a high level of mental competence among today's transescent youth. However, those responsible for directing development of intelligence cannot ignore the nature of the learner and must realize they might be entailing sacrifice to the mental health and to the behavior of those being educated.

In this context, the nature of the transescent learner has been the focal point of discussion throughout this chapter. It appears from the voluminous clinical research of Professor Piaget and his colleagues that mental development occurs in a constantly expanding sequence with present intellectual development being dependent upon previous development. This being the case, it is not reasonable to conclude that educators can successfully provide accelerated learning experiences which by-pass intermediate, necessary stages of development. Bruner[27] emphasizes this belief:

What is most important for teaching basic concepts is that the child be helped to pass progressively from concrete thinking to the utilization of more conceptually adequate modes of thought. But it is futile to attempt this by presenting formal explanations based on a logic that is distant from the child's manner of thinking and sterile in its implications for him.

Thus, what seems feasible and necessary is to conduct a careful analysis of content areas in an effort to discern the concepts involved; these concepts can be presented in a manner commensurate with transescent stage characteristics, even though they do not follow a traditional subject area format.

Another factor to consider is what the environmental effect is on the rate and stage of intellectual development. Piaget suggests that mental growth is similar to a biological process in which the organi-

---

27 Jerome Bruner, *The Process of Education* (Cambridge, Mass.: Harvard University Press, 1962), p. 38.

zational structures develop by assimilating experiences and then accommodating the results of these experiences into further mental structures. The richness of the experiences to which a learner is exposed appears to have a direct relation to the rate and extent of his cognitive development.

CHAPTER IV

Cultural Forces

The central theme permeating Chapters II and III was the changing status of the transescent and the resulting demands for a different life role brought about by these changes. Physically, the transescent undergoes dynamic changes. Mentally, the transescent moves from an understanding of the real and the concrete to an ability to relate to the theoretical and hypothetical. In this chapter, the focal point of discussion will be the transescent's evolving social status.

In the present decade there are cultural forces in existence which have deep implications for education at all levels, including the middle school years. In any attempt to restructure the educational process, one must take into consideration the nature of the cultural force as well as its interaction with similar representative forces; education of youth has little significance apart from the realities of environment. Realistically, it is not possible to assess our culture in *all* its diverse complexities; however, certain forces which impinge on education and youth can be explored meaningfully.

As in all age groups, the transescent youngster, too, has roots firmly imbedded in the nature of the culture in which he is developing. Anthropologist Margaret Mead, in her monumental study of the Samoan culture, clearly demonstrates the importance of this relationship. Little attempt is made here to develop intricate cross-cultural comparisons; nevertheless, Mead's[1] findings in Samoa are helpful when trying to understand the transescent in America. Mead discusses the cultural-growth relationship of Samoan children in this way:

> Is adolescence a period of mental and emotional distress for the growing girl as inevitably as teething is a period of misery for the small baby? Can we think of adolescence as a time in the life history of every girl which carries with it symptoms of conflict and stress. . . . Following the Samoan girls through every aspect of their lives

[1] Margaret Mead, *Coming of Age in Samoa* (New York: William Morrow and Company, 1928, 1955, 1961 by Margaret Mead), p. 196.

we have tried to answer this question, and we found throughout that we had to answer it in the negative. The adolescent girl in Samoa differed from her sister who had reached puberty in one chief respect, that in the older girl certain bodily changes were present which were absent in the younger girl. There were no other great differences to set off the group passing through adolescence from the group which would become adolescent in two years or the group which had become adolescent two years before.

If storm and stress are not natural companions of transescence, as Mead's study appears to indicate, why do youngsters in the United States often, certainly not always, derive emotional and social problems at this stage in their lives? Again, it is helpful to look at the Samoan culture through the eyes of Mead. In the following passage, Mead[2] describes the Samoan way of life from which one is able to deduce reasons for there being transescent stress in a complex industrial society:

> The Samoan background which makes growing up so easy, so simple a matter, is the general casualness of the whole society. For Samoa is a place where no one pays very high prices, no one suffers for his convictions or fights to death for special ends. Disagreements between parent and child are settled by the child's moving across the street, between man and his village by the man's removal to the next village, between husband and his wife's seducer by a few fine mats. Neither poverty nor great disasters threaten the people to make them hold their lives dearly and tremble for continued existence. No implacable gods, swift to anger and strong to punish, disturb the even tenor of their days. . . . No one is hurried along in life or punished harshly for slowness of development. Instead the gifted, the precocious, are held back until the slowest among them have caught the pace. Love and hate, jealousy and revenge, sorrow and bereavement are all matters of weeks. From the first months of its life, when the child is handled carelessly from one woman's hands to another's, the lesson is learned of not caring for one person greatly, not setting high hopes on any one relationship.

Obviously, the Samoan and American cultures have little in common, as each, of necessity, reacts to the demands of their respective societies. Nevertheless, in contrast, several points appear significant and will form the basis for discussion of the transescent in an American cultural context. First, the security base found in the primitive household is a broad one, not extremely dependent on a few indi-

2 *Ibid.,* pp. 198–199.

viduals, as is the case with the American family. Secondly, in the preindustrial society, there does not appear to be an either/or proposition in the maturing process, such as exists in America, by which the youngster is often considered either a child or an adult. This factor may be one of the reasons for the emergence of youth subcultures in the United States. Finally, the demands of the Samoan culture are not bound extensively to economic or political pressures so prevalent in the United States.

As Mead has inferred, a complex society impinges on the child in diverse ways—all filled with potential emotional and social problems. Thus at this point, it seems wise to examine these factors more extensively and to assess their importance for a middle school educational model.

The Family and the Transescent

In early stages of transescence, the youngster depends largely on his parents and home for personal security, interests, and values. It is during this period that the transescent begins to transfer his security base to the peer group. By the mid-teens this transfer assumes formidable proportions.

There is evidence indicating that by the time boys and girls reach their mid- and late-teens they constitute a society of peers depending largely on the interests and values of each other for personal security. Spaulding[3] cites this point of view in a perspective manner:

> . . . during the last twenty years a growing list of careful research projects in various fields of social relationships has suggested that within the secondary society certain types of at least quasi-primary groupings tend to appear and to become for their members very important devices for adaptation to their social milieu.

Seemingly, in later adolescence, the peer group has assumed relatively strong interdependence. This affinity for friend, as opposed to family, is in marked contrast to the child-home relationship during the period marking the last stages of childhood reported by Gesell, Ilg, and Ames.[4] They write:

> If ever the word family acquires its true meaning, it is when the child is ten years of age. Ten not only accepts but likes his lot. In

---

[3] C. B. Spaulding, "Cliques, Gangs, and Networks," *Sociology and Social Research*, XXXII (1950), 298.

[4] Gesell, Ilg, and Ames, *op. cit.*, p. 54.

fact no other father or mother seem to surpass his in his own eyes. ... This is the last age for some time to come when the child enters into a family excursion with casual thoughtfulness, adaptability and full enjoyment.

The American family is a conjugal unit in which the children arc associated mainly with their parents and siblings. Unlike the Samoan culture in which children depend upon relatives and friends in the intimate surrounds of the large household, American transescent security is centered primarily on interaction with parents. The American family has been characterized as "an island of emotional intimacy in a sea of strangers."[5]

This reliance on parents for security does not necessarily mandate that there will be adjustment problems for the transescent, but the possibility that this security base, by its very nature, may cause the transescent to make a poor environmental adjustment is strongly prevalent. Toby[6] provides a substantive analysis of this possibility:

> The small conjugal family system characteristic of industrial societies tends to make children highly dependent on their parents. Other sources of emotional support are not readily available. Nonetheless, the expectation is that the family into which one is born will disintegrate. Children remain dependent throughout life. They must leave the nest. The expectations surrounding occupational choice and the establishment of a family of one's own (family of procreation) create pressures to be more independent. During adolescence these two forces meet head-on; the structurally fostered dependence of an isolated family system and the independence required by a dynamic society. The turmoil of adolescence in industrial societies is largely due to the collision of these incompatible forces.

The process by which a youngster moves from a dependent to an independent status is a process of emancipation and is related to our culture. Parsons[7] states in this regard:

> It is at this point of emergence into adolescence that a set of patterns and behavior phenomena which involves a highly complex combination of age, grading, and sex role elements begin to develop. These may be referred to together as the phenomena of the

[5] Toby, op. cit., p. 337.
[6] Ibid., pp. 338–339.
[7] Talcott Parsons, "Age and Sex in the Social Structure of the United States," American Sociological Review, VII (1942), 604–616.

"youth culture." Certain of its elements are present in pre-adolescence and others in adult culture. But the peculiar combination in connection with this particular age level is unique and highly distinctive of American society.

The success or failure of emancipation appears closely related to the action of adults. This parental role is often difficult in that it entails a reversal of attitude. Kuhlen[8] points out:

> Parents who have long exercised authority over their children must learn to transfer that authority to them, and to accord the adolescent the equal status in the family of an adult who has as much right to make his decisions as has the parent himself. For many parents, learning these things represents a significant and not too easy readjustment.

The striking fact that transescents are capable of assuming responsibility is well exemplified: youngsters of this age grouping fought as freedom fighters in the Hungarian uprisings against the communists. Yet adults often overlook this capacity in transescents. They often relegate them to a position either of being too old for childish acts or too young for responsible action. There is a tendency for parents to be inconsistent in their relations with the emerging transescent, thereby creating confusion in the youngster's outlook. It is interesting to note one teenager's reaction as a participant in the Purdue Opinion Poll reported by Remmers and Radler.[9] This girl relates:

> One problem that I have is: I wish my parents would stop telling me one moment that I am grown up and to stop acting like a child and then the next instant when I would like to do something on my own they tell me that I am still a minor and have to do as they tell me.

Of course, the position of the parents is a difficult one—requiring much patience and understanding. When understanding parental attitudes are coupled with a stable home environment, emancipation is able to take place with a minimum of stress. With regard to this role of the home and parents, it is helpful to investigate some of the variables complicating the parent-child relationship in our society.

One important factor is the disparity of ages between parent and child. Punke[10] in an earlier study discovered that ages of fathers of

---

[8] Kuhlen, *op. cit.,* p. 581.

[9] H. H. Remmers and D. H. Radler, *The American Teenager* (New York: The Bobbs-Merrill Company, Inc., 1957), p. 94.

[10] H. H. Punke, "High School Youth and Family Quarrels," *School and Society,* LVIII (1943), pp. 507–511.

high school students were distributed in the following range: 30 percent under 42 years of age; 57 percent between 42 and 56 years of age; and 13 percent were 57 years or older. The mothers' ages ranged as follows: 54 percent under 42 years of age; 42 percent between 43 and 56 years; and 4 percent were 57 years or older. In our rapidly changing culture, this age gap seems to create a problem in the socializing function of the family—one which is not easily reconciled.

Davis[11] explains Figure 4 in this way:

> Because the birth-cycle interval persists throughout their conjoint life, parent and child are always at a different stage of development and their relations are always therefore potentially subject to conflict. E. G., when the parent is at stage D, the child is at stage B. But social change adds another source of conflict, for it means that the parent, when at the stage where the child now is, acquired a different cultural content from that which the child must now acquire at that stage. This places the parent in the predicament of trying to transmit old content no longer suited to the offspring's needs in a changed world. In a changing society, they do not, yet the parent tries to apply the content of A, B, C, etc. to the corresponding stages in the child's development, A', B', C', etc., which supposedly and actually have a different content. Thus, a constant (the birth-cycle) and a variable (social change) combine to produce parent-youth conflict.

Davis[12] schematically expresses the locus of this problem in Figure 5:

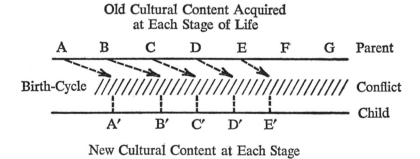

Figure 4. The Birth-cycle, Social change, and Parent-child Relations at Different Stages of Life.

---

[11] Kingsley Davis, "The Sociology of Parent-Youth Conflict," *American Sociological Review* (August, 1940), 523–535.
[12] *Ibid.*

Davis' reasoning seems applicable not only to parents but also to educators and other adults intimately associated with youth.

Another major factor, one alluded to previously, is the emotional relationship imbedded in the conjugal family. The close relationship of the parent and child is worthy of consideration in view of the potential instabilities of this arrangement. Parsons[13] elaborates on this emotional involvement:

> Since the effective kinship unit is normally the small conjugal family, the child's emotional attachments to kin are confined to relatively few persons instead of being distributed more widely. Especially important, perhaps, is the fact that no other adult woman has a role remotely similar to that of the mother. Hence, the average intensity of affective development in family relations is likely to be high. Secondly, the child's relations outside the family are only to a small extent ascribed. Both in the play group and in the school he must to a large extent "find his own level" in competition with others. Hence the psychological significance of his security within the family is heightened.

Seemingly, conditions interfering with the marital roles of the mother or father tend to affect the emotional security of the transescent and subsequently the emancipation process. Research studies support this view. Scarpatti, Murray, Dinitz, and Reckless[14] report that nondelinquent boys from intact homes enjoy a mutual acceptance with their parents. Conversely, Glueck and Glueck[15] confirmed that delinquent boys often come from homes which have undergone parental divorce, separation, desertion, or parental death.

In the United States, the father by economic necessity often must be absent from the home, leaving a majority of the child rearing responsibility to the mother. The approach used in this maternal responsibility has implications for transescent behavior. Giving insight is Levy's[16] discourse concerning maternal excesses:

> Theoretically, a sharp contrast may be drawn between overprotecting mothers who dominate and those who indulge. The former

[13] Talcott Parsons, "The Kinship System of the Contemporary United States" in *Social Perspectives on Behavior,* ed. Herman D. Stein and Richard A. Cloward (New York: The Free Press of Glencoe, Inc., 1958), pp. 14–15.

[14] F. R. Scarpatti, E. Murray, S. Dinitz, and W. C. Reckless, "The 'Good' Boy in a High Delinquency Area: Four Years Later," *American Sociological Review,* XXV (1960), 555–558.

[15] S. Glueck and E. T. Glueck, *Unraveling Juvenile Delinquency* (Cambridge, Mass.: Harvard University Press and The Commonwealth Fund, 1950), p. 280.

[16] David M. Levy, "Maternal Overprotection," *Psychiatry,* 2:563–597; *see* pp. 566–567.

express to the fullest degree that phase of maternal love that corresponds to possession of the love object. . . . Both exceed the usual parental overvaluation of the child. The former, however, attempt to constrict its personality, to trim it to the desired shape; the latter allow the child's personality to expand, giving luxuriant growth to infantile tendencies. The behavior problems of the children are constantly rebellious and aggressive in indulgent overprotection. . . . In a milder form such variation in parental response is typical of family life in general.

The father's absence may also affect the transescent's sex identity. Burton and Whiting[17] have proposed the "status envy hypothesis" thus:

> . . . persons will identify with models who control resources they covet. Boys from father-absent households, where the mother's status is particularly likely to be envied, are shown to experience considerable cross-sex identity conflict. The theory suggests that some delinquent acts of boys in gangs may be exaggerated expressions of masculine behavior resulting from conflict in sex identity.

In a related study of 225 boys, McCord, McCord, and Thurber[18] found that feminine aggressive behavior results from paternal absence and that the middle years of childhood may be a crucial factor in boys' sex role conflicts.

Unfortunately, in our society, the prevalence of unstable home environments seem greater in lower class homes. Toby[19] verifies this by stating:

> . . . family disorganization is much more concentrated among population elements poorly integrated into urban industrial society. For instance, more of the Negro population belong to the non-industrial out-group, which creates greater family instability among Negroes.

The lower socio-economic level creates many hazards for the transescent. In previous discussion (1) the adverse effects of poor nutrition on physical development; (2) the strained impact brought about by a lack of stimulating experience and opportunity on men-

---

[17] Roger V. Burton and John M. Whiting, "The Absent Father and Cross-Sex Identity" *Merrill-Palmer Quarterly of Behavior and Development,* VII (1961), 85–95.

[18] Joan McCord, William McCord, and Emily Thurber, "Some Effects of Paternal Absence on Male Children," *Journal of Abnormal and Social Psychology,* LXIV (1962), 361–369.

[19] Toby, *op. cit.,* p. 182.

tal growth; and (3) home instability have been noted as factors combining to force the educator of impoverished transescents to face a significant (but not impossible) challenge. Jones[20] cites what opportunities the school has to aid these children in the emancipation process:

> First, it [the school] can help in the process of emancipation from the home. It can sponsor activities which are accepted by the home but which depend only loosely upon parental sanction and practically not at all upon parental supervision. Next, it can introduce the child to the adult world better than the home can. Not only does it provide contact with many adults but vicariously—through study, literature, athletic contests, field work, and field trips—it can give the young person an appreciation of what is going on both in the community and in the world at large.

The Culture and the Transescent

The child's relations to others undergoes change with maturity. A young child's interests are largely self-centered, but as transescence approaches, interests in the peer group begin to be asserted in ever greater measure. To some degree, peer involvement is characteristic of all societies; however, in the American culture, it seems to hold a higher priority. This priority often presents problems for the emerging youngster. Toby[21] relates:

> In all societies, children are taught to interact with peers. In American society, however, peer socialization presents special difficulties: (1) In the United States, as in other industrial societies, the isolation of the conjugal family and the anonymity of the urban community accentuate the qualitative differences between relationships inside and outside the family. (2) In the United States more than in other industrial societies of the contemporary world; ideological pressure for "adjusting" to peers is well nigh inescapable. A youngster who lives in a world of books or dreams is forced by the expectations of his parents and of other adults in the community to come to terms with his peers—sometimes at the cost of his individuality.

---

[20] R. Stewart Jones, "Growing up in the Modern World" in *Adolescence*, eds. Ann E. Jewett and Clyde Knapp (Washington, D.C.: The Yearbook of the American Association for Health, Physical Education and Recreation, 1962), p. 23.
[21] Toby, *op. cit.*, p. 337.

On occasion observers of the American scene have described the emphasis on socialization and adjustment as excessive. Riesman's[22] opinion is of this nature:

> While the inner-directed parent frequently forced the pace of the child in its home setting, as for example, in cleanliness and toilet training habits, the outer-directed parent, more apt to be permissive in such matters, forces the pace, with like impatience, in the child's social life, though often hardly aware of doing so. Parents today are the stage managers for the meetings of three- and four-year olds, just as, in earlier eras, the adults managed marriages. Hence while "self-demand" feeding schedules are gaining ground for infants, self-demand is not observed when it comes to socialization outside the home. The daily schedule is an effort, with mother as chauffeur and booking agent, to cultivate all the currently essential talents, especially the gregarious ones. It is inconceivable to some supervising adults that a child might prefer his own company or that of just one other child.

With this cultural condition as a point of departure, it seems advisable to evaluate contemporary transescent interests. Transescence is characterized by a greater interest in one's own sex. Although there is a paucity of research relative to peer interests in this regard, studies, which have been undertaken, tend to confirm that at this age attitudes toward same-sex peers apparently are more reinforcing than attitudes involving opposite sex peers. Harris and Tseng[23] measured attitudes of boys and girls in this respect. They report with regard to boys:

> Approximately 65 to 70 percent of the boys give positive responses to other boys at all grade levels. Boys are more positive to boys than to girls in all grades. In general, taking into account the proportion of neutral attitudes, boys in the intermediate grades are more favorably than unfavorably disposed to girls. . . . By grade 8, about the same percentage of boys give favorable as give unfavorable responses to girls. . . . This finding does not bear out the general expectation of boys' heterosexual attitudes in adolescence.

Commenting on both sexes these same authors[24] relate, "Both sexes give more negative responses to opposite sex than to own sex."

---

[22] David Riesman, *The Lonely Crowd: A Study of the Changing American Character* (New Haven, Conn.: Yale University Press, 1950), p. 70.

[23] D. B. Harris and S. C. Tseng, "Children's Attitudes Toward Peers and Parents as Revealed by Sentence Completion," *Child Development*, XXVIII (1957), 404.

[24] *Ibid.*, p. 106.

With similar results, Meyer[25] investigated 387 pupils, 212 girls and 175 boys in grades 5 through 12 in a rural New York setting. This researcher stated:

> This study supports the hypothesis that same-sex social interactions are perceived by preadolescent and adolescent children as more reinforcing than social interactions with the opposite sex. The hypothesis that the difference between boys' and girls' perceptions of their own sex and opposite sex remains constant was upheld in the succorance-need ratings of both sexes. The hypothesis was again upheld in the boys' ratings of their own sex and opposite sex for the playmirth situation. However, the girls' ratings in the playmirth situation showed that after grade 7, girls perceived boys as increasingly more capable of satisfying their playmirth needs although they still prefer female companions.

During transescence relations to same-sex peers is a predominant feature of peer involvement. Significantly, however, the trend, which was evident in the phenomena of earlier physical maturation, toward earlier interests in the opposite sex is also discernible. In this vein, Landis[26] cites a few interesting statistics regarding marriage. He states, "In 1890, the average age at first marriage for men was 26.1 and for women 22.0. This year (1955) the average age at first marriage will be around 22.5 for men and slightly over 20 years for women." He further discloses from a California group studied the following data:[27]

> Ninety percent of the 205 senior high schools had had one or more student marriages during the previous year. One hundred forty-three had had student marriages in the tenth grade, 163 in the eleventh grade, and 173 in the twelfth grade. On a percentage basis 2.4 percent of sophomore girls, 4.0 percent of junior girls and 5.7 percent of senior girls had married.

By late transescence, a growing percentage of youngsters have dated. Smith[28] reports that 16 percent of the boys and 22 percent of the girls have dated at age 12; 29 percent of the boys and 46 per-

25 William J. Meyer, "Relationships Between Social Need Strivings and the Development of Heterosexual Affiliations," *The Journal of Abnormal and Social Psychology*, LIX (1959), 51–57.

26 J. T. Landis, "Attitudes and Policies Concerning Marriages Among High School Students," *Marriage and Family Living*, XVIII (1956), 128.

27 *Ibid.*, p. 129.

28 W. M. Smith, "Rating and Dating," *Marriage and Family Living*, XIV (1952), 313.

cent of the girls have dated by age 13; and 49 percent of the boys and 83 percent of the girls have dated by age 15.

In a study comparing attitudes and interests of three ninth grade classes in the same school but at time intervals of 18 and 24 years (1935, 1953, 1959), Jones[29] found a greater maturity of heterosexual interests in the later year classes than in 1935.

Similarly, in studies over the past two decades, Kuhlen[30] discovered a comparable pattern of earlier heterosexual relationships.

Harris[31] made a comparative study in students' interests related to love and marriage. Encompassing the years from 1935 to 1957 the study's results have been put to significant use. The author contributed changing interest patterns to changing cultural conditions. He[32] writes, "Today youth marry younger and show an earlier interest in social relations, love and marriage. Our culture appears to recognize more openly now than two decades ago the sex, love, and marriage problems of young people."

In our culture, the relationship of sex interests has further significance since we expect people to assume different patterns of belief and actions at different stages in their lives. Physiologically capable of sexual activity, a youngster faces severe restrictions in showing any interest toward using this potential while he is in the transescent or adolescent periods of life. Benedict[33] calls attention to this cultural aspect:

> The contrast with arrangements in our culture is very striking and against this background of social arrangements in other cultures the adolescent period of "Sturm and Drang" with which we are so familiar becomes intelligible in terms of our discontinuous cultural institutions and dogmas rather than in terms of physiological necessity.

Again, earlier physiological maturation tends to make the period

---

[29] Mary C. Jones, "A Comparison of the Attitudes and Interests of Ninth Grade Students over Two Decades," *Journal of Educational Psychology,* LI (1960), 175–186.

[30] R. G. Kuhlen and B. J. Lee, "Personality Characteristics and Social Acceptability in Adolescence," *Journal of Educational Psychology,* XXXIV (1943), 326.

[31] Dale B. Harris, "Sex Differences in the Life Problems and Interests of Adolescents, 1935 and 1957," *Child Development,* XXX (1959), 453–459.

[32] *Ibid.,* p. 458.

[33] Ruth Benedict, "Continuities and Discontinuities in Cultural Conditioning" in *Social Perspectives in Behavior,* ed. Herman D. Stein and Richard A. Cloward (New York: The Free Press of Glencoe, Inc., 1958), p. 247.

of sexual restraint longer and more difficult. Nonetheless, in our society with its socio-economic pressures created by a technological era, this situation appears inherent.

Despite this increased sexual awareness, founded on physiological maturation, students in transescence receive very little adult attention in matters of human growth or sexual development.

In an earlier study, Ramsey[34] discovered that initial sexual information was obtained from other boys in the peer group in greater proportion than was furnished by either parent. Angelo and Mech[35] in a recent survey of 67 females at Oklahoma University disclose:

> . . . the efforts of parents and the school are not very heavy, at least with respect to acting as an "initial" source of sex information. It would appear that with exception of menstruation, girls received most of their sex information from their companions and from "printed matter."

The girls involved at Oklahoma University expressed a desire for earlier sex instruction and they further believed that a course for parents would be helpful. In our culture, seemingly, this is an area to which little attention is given at a time when a great emphasis is needed.

Cultural conditions impinging on transescents, causing earlier patterns of interests and experiences, continue to change rapidly. These changes have deep implications for the educational administrator who must create an educational environment commensurate with the changes. Thomas[36] points this out in the following manner:

> Change in any field produces certain stresses and the old pattern is thrown out of balance. To adapt necessitates readjustments. When change is of the revolutionary order, change is always difficult, and friction results before a workable pattern is evolved that will prove acceptable.

In a comparable way, Symonds[37] emphasizes the same position by stating, "Change the social and economic structure of society and

[34] G. V. Ramsey, "The Sex Information of Younger Boys," *American Journal of Orthopsychiatry,* XIII No. 2 (April, 1943), 347–352.

[35] H. Angelo and E. V. Mech, "Some 'First' Sources of Sex Information as Reported by Sixty-seven College Women," *Journal of Psychology,* XXXIX (1955), 323.

[36] Maurice Thomas, *Education and a Productive Society: Horace Mann Lecture* (Pittsburgh: University of Pittsburgh Press, 1953), p. 26.

[37] P. M. Symonds, "Sex Differences in the Life Problems and Interests of Adolescents," *School and Society,* XLIII (1936), 751–752.

you immediately change the relative emphasis of these problems and interests."

Over a period of approximately two decades, interests and attitudes have shown a definite earlier trend. The most plausible factors responsible for this trend arc (1) earlier maturation as discussed in Chapter II, and (2) cultural changes which have permeated the American scene during the post-World War II years. It seems helpful to assess, at least in a broad way, some of these changing cultural facets and their implications for transescents.

Gow, Holzner and Pendleton[38] summarize American cultural change in this way:

> In the United States the transition involves the following aspects: continued urbanization, with the growth of mammoth metropolitan agglomerations and changes in the nature of city life; the growth of complex and interlocking organizations in the public and private domains, accompanied by increasingly organized regulation of social life; greater homogeneity of the population through a redistribution of wealth, the relative decline of ethnic stratification and a decline in the polarization of the social classes; increasing similarity between the great regions of America and an enormous increase in the interdependence of the whole nation in the political, economic and cultural fields. All of this has resulted in the development of new patterns of social stratification which determines the life chances of individuals and require different kinds of skills for successive participation in the society, thus affecting directly every person.

The concomitants of societal changes appear to have multiple implications for transescence. The materialistic by-products of our age, such as mass media, modes of travel, and means of communication, are providing opportunities for increased experiences, intellectual and social, unrivaled in history. For example, students are instantaneously and dramatically exposed to the events of the technological era (such as outer space exploration) in a few hours of television viewing. The fantastic prognosis for learning is underlined by Sarnoff[39] when he predicts, "Science and Technology will advance more in the next thirty-six years than in all the millennia since man's creation." Conversely, the effect of these rapid changes tends to widen the gulf between child and adult, complicating the

---

[38] Gow, Holzner, and Pendleton, *op. cit.*, p. 168.
[39] David Sarnoff, "By the End of the Twentieth Century," *Fortune,* LXIX (1964), 116.

kind of relationship needed for successful emancipation. It not only affects the child but also affects the parent. Kuhlen[40] remarks, "To-day many adults are experiencing something of the confusion that might be expected to face an adolescent who, with little pertinent experience to guide him, is confronted by inconsistent demands."

Another two edged sword for transescents is found in the geographic mobility of Americans wherein many transescents are faced frequently with new environments. White[41] comments, "Men in the twenty-five-to-thirty-four age group are only 7.5 percent of the total population but they account for 12.4 percent of the migration." He further cites:[42]

> Even companies reporting no increase in the number of times each individual moves report an increase in the sheer number of men being moved. G. E. has compared a cross section of its forty-five-year old executives with one of its thirty-five-year olds. In the ten years after they were twenty-five, 42 percent of the older group had moved at least once; during the same age period, 58 percent of the younger group had moved.

Add to this list the movement of armed forces personnel, migrant workers, and interurban families and the enormity of geographic relocation is apparent. Studies showing the average age when men marry and studies showing when most men relocate lead to the conclusion that the transescent is a highly mobile student. A new environment provides the transescent with valuable experiences that can be gained through interaction with different localities. On the other hand, it often provides a period of instability, at a crucial time in which peer associates are becoming increasingly important to him. Coleman[43] remarks about this, "The simple fact that adolescents are looking to each other rather than to the adult community for their social rewards has a number of significant implications."

Another factor, intricately involved with changes going on in our society, is the growing transescent and adolescent economic market. Our culture exerts an economic influence which capitalizes on the nature of our youngsters and influences their behavior. Transes-

---

[40] Kuhlen, *op. cit.,* p. 169.
[41] William H. White Jr., *The Organization Man* (New York: Simon and Schuster, 1956), p. 269–270.
[42] *Ibid.*
[43] James S. Coleman, *The Adolescent Society* (New York: Cromwell-Collier Publishing Co., 1961), p. 11.

cents, being very much aware of the opinion of their peers and in need of social reinforcement provided by this opinion, in large degree, tend to be conformists. Fads revolving around appearance, dress, or popular music are always in vogue—most transescents want to be a part of the current fad. This characteristic is the basis for an enormous economic market. Norder[44] verifies this contention:

> In Metropolitan areas, entire merchandising programs are built around the teen-age market, for advertisers know that youth are susceptible to suggestion. Because adolescents typically want to look alike and talk alike, the huckster's cries pay off with youngsters.

Occasionally, educators have taken issue with these personal type fads, citing the detrimental effect that excessively tight trousers, short skirts, excessive make-up, or any similar fad has on the learning situation. When this happens, the transescent is caught between the conflicting ideologies of the economic push, of adult standards, and of peer approval. The dilemma forces the transescent to adopt a position. If he conforms to the fad, he risks authoritative displeasure and pressure; if he gives in to adult standards, he risks peer rejection. This situation is not unlike many other situations generated by changing cultural conditions. The transescent educator is challenged to take action—the wisdom he uses will either enhance or retard the educational process. There is a definite need for individualistic thought in a dynamic society. The 1959 Regional Commission on Interrelationships of Secondary Schools, Colleges and Professional Schools held at the University of Pittsburgh[45] commented on this as follows:

> An individual fulfills himself and realizes himself as a human being by developing intellectual and moral integrity. A person so characterized is able to think independently and critically and is ready and willing to make his own value judgements. Our society must have a liberal leavening of such persons if it is to have the vigor, wisdom and morale to confront successfully the challenges it is likely to face in the future. Individualism in this sense is essential to survival of a free society.

---

[44] H. Orville Norder, "Social Pressures Influencing Adolescent Behavior," *California Journal of Secondary Education*, XXIX (1954), 357.

[45] Charles H. Peake *et al.*, "Social Relations Symposium," *Today's Leaders Look at Tomorrow's Learning: Regional Commission on Interrelationships of Secondary Schools, Colleges and Professional Schools* (Pittsburgh: University of Pittsburgh, 1959), p. 4.

Our contemporary society, however, abounds in pressures to conform not only in overt behavior but in thought and judgement. The individual is encouraged from all sides to parrot the thinking of others and to depend uncritically on the collective judgement to accept something as right or wrong, wise or foolish, because "everybody" says so, to value what others value and to disdain what others reject. Mass media, the amorphous "they" make it all too easy for the individual to abdicate his personal responsibility to think, to judge and to decide. Making thoughtful judgements and accepting personal responsibility for the consequences of decisions are forms of maturity and of anguish.

The impact of diverse elements—some demanding conformity others requiring individuality—is a deep and necessary concern the transescent educator has to meet.

Implications for Education

In society the transescent develops toward maturity through interaction with the cultural environment. Environment is an external force to which a youngster has to adapt even though the force is largely uncontrollable by him. To what degree of success the transescent adjusts to his environment affects his personal development as well as the development of society.

In the earlier chapters, when discussing the socio-psychological model, it was found that the biological development of youth in the past century had undergone a significant trend toward earlier physical and mental maturation in relation to chronological age. This phenomenon, due largely to highly favorable socio-economic factors, presently shows little indication of abating. Culturally, a comparable trend is evident. Interests and attitudes previously attributed to later in life are emerging earlier. Since this pattern is imbedded in a favorable cultural era, it is likely that this trend also will continue as long as opportunities for enriched experiences accelerate and occasions for broader peer involvement, through technological developments, increase.

As democracy's medium for the transmission of cultural values, education must alter basic patterns, if it is to carry out its inherent role effectively. Alterations must be based on the nature of the learner as well as on the expectations and demands of society. Therefore, the educator must consider (1) that the physical factor of maturing at an earlier age has created personal needs challenging youth's security, and (2) that the impact of a significantly changing culture has put tremendous demands on youth which cannot be met, as in the agrarian society, simply by learning a body of facts. Rather, it is imperative that transescents learn life processes based on understanding, adjustment, and control of rapid change (in order to interact with a constantly emerging way of life). To accomplish this, transescent educators must be willing to investigate the worth of and alter, if necessary, educational approaches previously considered fundamental. Traditional approaches might have been successful in meeting the needs of youth in an agrarian and even in a heavy industrial society, but they cannot meet the requirements of a dynamic era. Alterations must come in a manner which will not negate the basic democratic ideals rooted in earlier American culture, and they must be approached with the realization that there are pressures moving in or tending to reverse direction. Melby[46] comments:

> In America, where widespread education has been a foundation stone of freedom, the current attacks on our education seem hard to explain. When it comes to remedies proposed by the critics, it is a notable fact that most of them point in undemocratic directions such as a return to a rigid subject-matter curriculum, emphasis on the three R's rather than on citizenship and personality development, and special education for the gifted.

Certainly basic education is important, but a narrow rigid approach is not commensurate with the nature of the transescent nor the character of our present culture.

---

[46] Ernest O. Melby, *Education for Renewed Faith in Freedom* (Columbus, Ohio: The Ohio State University Press, 1959), pp. 3–4. Copyrighted and permission granted by Kappa Delta Pi.

CHAPTER V

Middle School Environment

In preceding chapters, a socio-psychological model was constructed based on the idiographic and nomothetic dimensions of transescent behavior. The vital elements in this model were those relating to the physical, intellectual, emotional, sociological, political, and economical areas of transescence.

The middle school educational model will be constructed in such a manner that an isomorphic relationship will form a conceptual link between the elements of the socio-psychological model and the middle school educational model.

The socio-psychological model (see Figure 1, Page 6) presents a composite of transescent behavior which has significance for a middle school environment. Educational climate is of vital concern, since whatever philosophy is adopted will have an influence on student behavior in all facets of school life. Although the concept of environment is intangible, it has an appreciable effect on everyone within the school; it is similar to the incidental music of a well directed motion picture whose purpose is to subtly create an appropriate mood for the audience. In like manner, the school's learning environment should foster curiosity, creativity, and independence, *or* it may stifle these desired attributes and covet conformity.

The learning environment suggested by the nature of transescence is one of flexibility—permitting students much freedom of action. Flexibility should foster independence in learning pursuits, but it does not imply that these need be chaos or a lack of restrictions. Certainly, administrative controls are necessary to insure student welfare, safety, and learning processes, but it must be remembered that the nature of the transescent is best served in an atmosphere of minimized rigidity.

In subsequent discussion, physical, mental, and cultural guideposts will be discussed (in an operational manner) in an effort to relate transescence to an appropriate learning environment. The cornerstone for these suggested guideposts will be the socio-psychological model.

Environmental Guidepost: The Relationship of Transescents' Physical Growth with the Middle School Environment

Transescence requires a close relationship between the student and the adult school staff. The transescent emancipation process obtains greatest success when an understanding and a friendly association exists between older and younger ages—made possible by a nonrigid school climate. If an atmosphere of friendliness prevails, transescents are able to seek adult advice vital to understanding their strange and rapid growth processes. For example, menstruation creates less anxiety for the girl who finds an atmosphere which permits friendly discussion of this occurrence with the teacher, nurse, secretary, or school counselor. Because trust is inherent to this type of approach, many opportunities should abound wherein transescents can accept responsibility for personal action necessary for the emancipation process.

Since a multitude of personal needs and emotional reactions are created by rapid physical growth and the accompanying physiological changes occurring (at stagnated intervals) in the lives of transescents, the learning environment should not stress physical standards and goals which can be attained only by the physically talented. Even though our culture places great emphasis on the physically outstanding person, the middle school should recognize the emotional dangers that face transescents who are incapable of meeting exceptional standards. Interscholastic athletics as well as newspaper contests selecting "Queens" or "Kings" should be avoided. Instead, well conducted intramural athletic programs and physical educational programs should be developed—in which all students can be successful in some way. These programs can not only assist necessary physical development but can provide opportunity for the majority of students to gain peer respect.

The school environment should minimize situations wherein emotional stress could be caused by students' physical growth differences. At a time when boys and girls are deeply concerned over a lack of maturation symbols, such as pubic hair or growth of external genital organs, it seems ill advised to force them into situations of mass exposure—one being that of "group" showers. Good health habits require bathing after vigorous activity; however, this can be accomplished in the privacy of individual cubicles.

The middle school climate should provide maximum opportunity for physical activity. A rigid atmosphere is incompatible with rapid growth. Therefore, transescent programs should emphasize physical movement rather than inactive proceedings. Since transescents, engulfed in accelerating physical growth, need exercise and outlets for emotional tension, the middle school should offer them many opportunities for physical activity both during and after school hours. Lengthy written homework assignments negate opportunities for physical activities. Therefore, if outside school assignments should be given. They should involve experimental activities—such as procuring stagnant pond water for the next day's science experiment, as one example.

Environmental Guidepost: The Relationship of Transescents' Mental Growth with the Middle School Environment

A flexible learning environment enhances stage level mental development. It has been indicated that experience is an essential ingredient for the growth of mental structures—through assimilation and mental accommodation. In a restrictive learning environment, experiences tend to be carefully selected by the staff for student consumption; however, in a flexible environment, youngsters are able to pursue personal curiosity, develop further interests, and increase opportunities for experience by means of a chain reaction effect, i.e., one experience providing the motivation for an additional experience. For example, if a student studying the culture of Canada were to become interested in the fur industry, a school climate should exist enabling this youngster to pursue this interest in a resource center—at the time of interest, not in a "later chaper" of the textbook.

Similarly, an educational atmosphere should allow students maximum access to the total school environment. There are instances in which the individual classroom does not possess resources necessary for pursuit of a current topic. When these occasions occur, students should, independent of other class members, have access to school-wide aids not present in the individual classroom—such as models, maps, charts, globes, television, radio, audio-visual aids, or resource books. These aids can greatly expand transescent learning experiences, providing they are used in a manner commensurate with transescence. If they are used merely as an extension of the traditional classroom lecture approach, they probably will add little in the way of new experiences; but if used in a resource manner, they have significant value. For example, transescents may study American foreign policy in Latin America by listening to a tape recording of the late President John F. Kennedy's Alliance for Progress proposal and find it quite beneficial.

Again, students in a rigid learning climate often are not provided with opportunities for independent movement from the classroom to a resource center. This lack of freedom not only tends to deprive the individual of a learning experience at a time most propitious for its success, but it also deprives the transescent of adult faith which is needed at a time when the emancipation process is escalating.

Relative to mental stage development, it is likely that some students will move from a concrete operations stage to a formal operations level of cognition. Stage level psychologists believe that when a movement to a new mental growth stage occurs, there is a period of heightened egocentrism, as the subject interacts within a new and untried area. They suggest further that the principal means of meeting this new challenge is through peer social interaction. Logically, an environment permitting social involvement is helpful to mental growth, while rigidity of rules and school patterns tends to inhibit the alleviation of egocentrism. In the classroom, teaching methods emphasizing a lecture format would seemingly have a similar effect. In earlier years, as youngsters advance from the preoperations level to a concrete operations mental stage, educators have successfully provided a learning environment emphasizing social interaction. Even though the transescent mental movement occurs at a more advanced level of cognition, the social interaction principle seems equally valid.

Finally, a learning environment conducive to mental growth should provide opportunities for relaxation from emotional pressures. There are occasions when transescents need to avoid vigorous academic pursuits. Emotional tensions occasionally need outlets which are not possible to attain in the rigid classroom except through deviant means; inflexibility negates necessary opportunities for assisting the youngster in this regard and the student feels compelled to be ill, truant, delinquent, or utilizes any number of escape mechanisms. If during periods of emotional or intellectual stress, the learning environment enabled transescents to relax independent of classroom protocol (by means of pursuits involving reading, use of resource centers, or other techniques), long range mental development could be enhanced.

Environmental Guidepost: The Relationship of Cultural Forces with Transescence in the Middle School Environment

The socio-psychological model indicates that the nature of American culture provides the transescent with maturation problems greater than those incurred solely through the physical growth processes. A flexible learning environment may assist in reducing culturally accentuated pressures felt by the transescent.

In this context, one of the problems faced by transescents revolves around the precarious security base of the conjugal family. For transescents, whose security base is dependent on their parents, a rigid learning atmosphere provides little additional security. In an atmosphere in which youngsters may relate easily with many school personnel, however, the security base is broadened and sole dependence on one or two adults is supplemented.

Since the evolving transescent considers the peer association important, it seems reasonable to expect a middle school to provide for this need. Socialization requires interaction and interaction requires a flexible climate. Since transescence is marked by a desire for contacts with same-sex peers even though there is a marked trend toward earlier opposite-sex involvement in our culture, an elastic climate will enable same-sex involvement in curricular and activity pursuits. By the same token, a middle school should provide limited opportunities for opposite-sex involvement by offering appropriate large group activities rather than by emphasizing the boy-girl relationship normally found in activities such as proms.

Early discussion indicated that transescents possess emotional and social problems coming out of our culture's emphases on physical growth; consequently, considerable anxiety is generated if menstruation or physical growth spurts fail to materialize. In a flexible school, grouping of transescents irrespective of chronological ages or grade levels may be accomplished. This capability would help reduce pressures on the slowly maturing child who might feel he has to keep social pace with the early maturer. On the other hand, where rapid physical growth occurs, this same capability would enable the emerging transescent to move in a group with more compatible interests.

International, political, and technological developments have had a "backlash" effect on the American school. This has resulted in academic pressures being brought on the transescent. Obviously, transescent educators cannot reduce world tensions or create an island of tranquility in a sea of pressure, but they can make adjustments which will reduce the impact of these forces. Pressures for college entrance and for "success" are so prevalent in our culture that this impact marks the transescent, even though college lies years in the future. It seems more plausible to treat transescents educationally at their own level rather than to insist on them mastering "college preparatory" courses in their middle school years. For example, instead of mastering one foreign language or a high school level mathematics course, it seems more realistic (in light of the emotional side effects) to provide transescents with immediate rather than remote academic goals.

Another significant advantage a flexible learning environment provides is the understanding and promulgation of American democracy. One of the principles of the formal operations level of cognition is the ability of the transescent to visualize the theoretical. Transescents possessing this capacity should interact in a learning climate exemplifying democracy. Since democracy entails many theoretical concepts which are difficult to learn vicariously, a school efficiently autocratic may find difficulty in transmitting democratic principles. Conversely, if transescents are constantly involved in making decisions relating to school life, there is an opportunity for them to comprehend democratic processes practically. This approach has additional value in that youngsters learn to accept personal responsibility so necessary for the emancipation process.

Inherent in a democracy is the principle of individual worth and rights. A school which lacks flexibility and which approaches most situations from the standpoint of administrative convenience teaches little respect for the individual. The fact that there are others who may want to go to the resource center at the same time, causing potential hall confusion, is no reason to deny a transescent this needed learning venture. The extent to which the administrative body of rules denies independent student needs is the extent to which individualism is negated, interests stifled, and intellectual curiosity rejected.

A transescent learning environment needs flexibility also in order to give youngsters the opportunity for understanding and being active participants in change. If changes are being contemplated in the school's format of socialization programs, assembly schedules, or activity offerings, transescents should be intimately involved in these alterations; for it is through this sort of involvement that youngsters have the opportunity to study causal factors necessitating changes and hopefully may acquire abilities that will help them adjust to subsequent change patterns.

CHAPTER VI

Educational Program

Since the middle school educational model necessitates an isomorphic relationship with the socio-psychological model, the proposals embodied in this chapter have their roots in the physical,
mental, emotional, and cultural characteristics of transescents. It is
conceivable that other educational theorists may arrive at different
conclusions based on the evidence presented in the first model;
nonetheless, in the opinion of the writer, the suggested educational
model is the gestalt most commensurate with the earlier model.

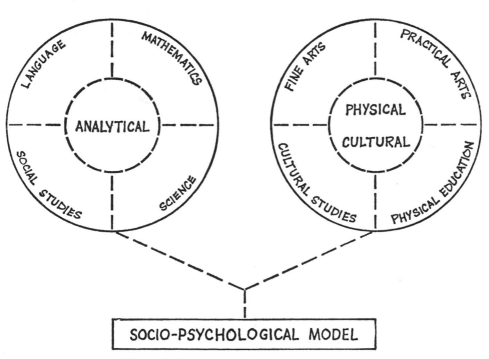

Figure 5. Middle School Curricula Structure.

Middle School Curricula

There are two proposed curricula in the educational model which will be termed analytical and physical-cultural. Figure 5 represents a schematic portrayal of these divisions in relation to the socio-psychological model.

Figure 5 indicates four content divisions in the analytical curriculum. These include language, mathematics, social studies, and science. These facets may be considered in both a separate as well as an interrelated context. The common elements creating curricular interrelations are the analytical thought processes inherent in each of the four content areas.

In the physical-cultural curriculum, there are also four content areas suggested by Figure 5: fine arts, physical education, practical arts, and cultural studies. In the case of these segments, however, there is an aspect of greater interrelatedness than was the character of the analytical division. As illustrated, each curricular structure is founded on the socio-psychological model; therefore, each has a relationship to each other.

As noted in Figure 5, the analytical curriculum includes as one of its components the social studies, while the physical-cultural curriculum contains the segment termed the cultural studies. Since there is similarity in terminology and content in these two areas, it is necessary to make a concise distinction in the educational model as to what the purpose of each area is.

In the social studies facet of the analytical curriculum, students will concentrate on an analysis of the skills and principles embodied in the content areas comprising the social studies. For example, in the analytical curriculum, students may analyze the relationship of geographic conditions with the industry of that region, or the impact of various diplomatic events on the outbreak of hostilities. In this way, emphasis in the analytical curriculum will be placed on the thought processes that are necessary for gaining a critical understanding of the social studies content areas.

The major function of the cultural studies facet of the physical-cultural curriculum is that of enabling students to gain a knowledge of the lives and activities of people within a given region or culture —as the basis for a physical-cultural unit. For example, in the study of Europe, students may examine the customs of Europeans; this serves as a foundation knowledge for a curriculum unit involving the fine arts, practical arts, and physical education phases of the physical-cultural curriculum.

While content in both the social studies and cultural studies areas will be similar, and, at times inseparable, the basic distinction is one of emphasis. This distinction will become more apparent as each of these curricula is discussed.

The paradigm in Figure 8 will be functionally expanded in terms of concepts involved in each of the curricula; however, a finite development of these curricula in terms of total curricular sequences is considered beyond the scope of this writing.

Physical-Cultural Curriculum

Transescence, a period in which physical growth with its attendant changes in interests and attitudes assumes formidable proportions, has led research scholars to describe this physical growth composite as the most vital educational concern of transescence. Therefore, it is essential that our educational structure include curricular provisions for meeting this need successfully.

Transescence, potentially a dynamic and satisfying stage in the growth and development of the child to maturity, is a period which cannot be ignored; nor can the philosophy that physical and interest changes of transescents be relegated to some other institution's responsibility be accepted. This philosophy would be tantamount to believing that the only import aspect of a medical operation is locating the organ to be removed and thinking the physical condition of the patient as irrelevant to the task of removal. In like manner, the whole physical condition of the youngster must be a basis upon which the physical-cultural curriculum centers.

The physical-cultural curriculum provides appreciable interrelatedness in the areas of the fine arts, practical arts, physical education, and the cultural facets of the social studies. This curricular approach seems plausible and feasible, relative to the socio-psychological model. As an illustration of this principle, a physical-cultural unit focusing on the culture of Japan may be suggested. Within this unit, curriculum content might include oriental art and music (fine arts); projects involving Japanese clothing, foods, crafts, and hobbies (practical arts); participation in sports, games, and dances (physical education); curriculum content relative to Japanese government, customs, and social institutions (cultural studies). Having various aspects of the culture form the basis of such a unit, content skills and understandings can be developed concurrently.

Within physical-cultural content groupings, curricular objectives should reflect this interrelatedness. For example, folk dancing activities may logically be associated with both physical education and the fine arts, while the study of a national holiday may involve customs—aspects of music, sports, and clothing attire. In effect, the totality of the culture permeates all content areas. This does not negate skill development normally associated with the various individual subject components; on the contrary, it should provide an increased motivational base for their development.

In this arrangement, flexible unit scheduling is a necessity for success. There will be limited occasions in which students may follow a segmented schedule similar to those in use in the traditional school. Figure 6 presents a schedule pattern of this type. Letters A, B, C, and D symbolize four intra unit groupings.

CURRICULAR AREAS				
Cultural Studies	Physical Education	Fine Arts	Practical Arts	Resource
A	B	C	D	
B	C	D	A	
C	D	A	B	
D	A	B	C	

Figure 6. Physical-Cultural Equal Time Interval Schedule.

In Figure 7, students in the various groupings attend sessions in equal time intervals. At these sessions, physical-cultural staff members can introduce, motivate, or stress the basic skills and understandings involved in the culture being studied.

An altered schedule pattern is presented in Figure 7. This sample schedule as opposed to Figure 6 will be the type of schedule generally employed.

CURRICULAR AREAS				
Cultural Studies	Physical Education	Fine Arts	Practical Arts	Independent Study
	C	D		
B	C + D		A	A + B
			A + B	A

Figure 7. Flexible Physical-Cultural Schedule.

Figure 7 exemplifies a schedule pattern with appreciable flexibility. Within the progression of a unit, individuals and groups quite often need varying time segments for the conduct of practical activities. As the need arises, various combinations of the flexible schedule shown in Figure 7 may be utilized.

For example: Groups C and D in Figure 7 may require the entire session for studying and practicing the intricate phases of a Japanese folk dance. At the same time, students in Group B are dividing their time between classroom cultural studies endeavors and independent study at the resource center. Group A transescents will be involved in practical arts activities with the exception of a few students who are permitted independent study.

It may be noted that within the framework of the flexible schedule, students are permitted to pursue an independent study program as the need arises. For example, while the majority of students in Group A may be working in the practical arts areas developing a model Japanese theatre scene, a few of their classmates may desire to go to the resource center to do research in the literature which will provide a more detailed description of the physical appearance of the oriental stage or the costumes of the actors. They should be allowed to do so.

An additional gain (realized after an analysis of Figure 7) exists in ability to combine separate groups for a learning episode. As an illustration, groups C and D may spend the first segment of the session as separate groups reviewing content facets of the folk dance;

later, the two groups combine. In such an instance, two content areas are involved—both from an individual and from an interrelated standpoint.

The physical-cultural curriculum is founded on numerous factors embodied in the socio-psychological model. In the following passages, these areas of relationship will be analyzed.

As transescents engage in the various learning processes, considerable peer interaction takes place by virtue of the very nature of the learning activities. Students preparing a committee report must make group decisions. Through the verbal interaction involved, transescents are afforded many opportunities for needed socialization. As stated previously, stage level psychologists believe the principal factor in freeing youngsters from intellectual disequilibrium, which appears at the onset of a more advanced stage of mental development, is social interaction.

The physical-cultural curriculum has been devised also to provide a more comprehensive base whereby transescents can gain peer approval. Presently in our culture, a boy's physical success is often related to his ability in "large muscle" activities; here the early maturer tends to excel. Although the late maturer is often more proficient in activities requiring agility and coordination, normally little curricular emphasis is placed on these traits. Consequently, the late maturer has few opportunities in which to gain needed peer respect. In most other world cultures, however, physical characteristics, such as agility and coordination, play an important role—in national sports, games, and dances. A physical-cultural unit involving sports of this nature can provide the late maturing transescent with opportunities for gaining needed peer approval. Similarly, late maturing girls can gain peer respect through the varied creative elements existing in the practical and fine arts of other cultures.

The middle school must also recognize the need transescents have in developing independence as they progress from a home-centered base of security to a security base involving peers. Envisioned in the physical-cultural curriculum are abundant possibilities for students to gain confidence necessary for this transition. These opportunities should not be limited to the gifted youngsters, but should be accessible to all. Through the curriculum transescents should be able to plan, research, or practice in an independent and responsible context, enabling the emancipation process to go on.

It is indicated in the socio-psychological model that transescents need a thorough understanding of personal growth processes. A physical-cultural curriculum seems to offer unique possibilities for meeting this need. Simply by the nature of the content areas involved, there are occasions for faculty-student contact in same-sex classes. Through this arrangement, staff members can spend considerable time in instructional discussions relating to growth developments and their implications for transescents.

The vital role which experiences play in transescent development receives added impetus in the physical-cultural curriculum. Particularly helpful in this direction is the study of various cultures. Although it is beneficial to study world cultures in a vicarious manner, experiencing cultural aspects in a physical context appreciably broadens these experiences. This is especially true in areas relating to the appreciation and understanding of people comprising the culture being studied.

Another paramount consideration for the transescent educator is realizing how important physical activity is in the lives of transescents. While daily programs should employ learning tasks in a manner insuring extensive physical exertion, the transescent's individual status must be carefully considered. There are periods in transescence, caused by rapid growth, illness, or emotional stress, during which physical activity could be detrimental and therefore should be temporarily curtailed. Conversely, in other cases, activity should be accelerated to meet individual needs.

Evaluation of student progress in the physical-cultural curriculum should be continuous and would be dependent upon curricular goals. It is suggested that student evaluation be reported to parents in the form of a series of faculty judgments relative to the individual's development. This would eliminate the determination of a passing or failing grade. Items relating to physical development, individual interests, socialization, cultural appreciation, emancipation, and creativity are not only difficult to grade, but in the process of making a letter grade, judgment may defeat the desirable outcomes sought by the curriculum.

Analytical Curriculum

In a culture which is in the midst of a knowledge explosion, the philosophy of instruction is important. Particularly perplexing is the question of emphasis when considering a course of action. Should emphasis be placed primarily on teaching a body of facts surrounding current knowledge, or should it be centered on the development of student thought processes? In view of the documentation found in the socio-psychological model, it seems more logical to devise a curriculum founded on the universality of mental thought processes. Of course, this should not eliminate consideration of the vast body of current knowledge; but, it does indicate that this body of knowledge should be utilized as the vehicle through which thought processes may be used to stimulate mental growth.

There are fundamental points regarding the stage level philosophy which have significance for the analytical curriculum. A primary consideration is the level of mental development which transescents have attained. Within the range of transescence, students will be involved in thought processes characteristic of concrete operations and formal operations mental stages. Thus, some youngsters are mentally operating in concrete or real terms, while others are able to interact cognitively in the theoretical or abstract.

It seems advisable in analytical curriculum construction to devise instructional content sequentially, ranging from the concrete to the theoretical. Relative to concrete operations, learning tasks which enable transescents to deal with the task from a nontheoretical standpoint should be incorporated. Progressively, learning tasks should be devised sequentially so that, as transescents accommodate and develop mental structures, they approach a learning task from the theoretical. For example, a sequential learning task in science relating to the effect of decreasing temperature on water may be constructed on the concrete operations end of the curriculum continuum by demonstrating that ice is formed at a temperature below 32 degrees fahrenheit. Conversely, a formal operations curricular task might explore the effects of ice on aircraft wings at high altitudes, or the impact which floods resulting from ice concentrations have on the economy.

The element of experience assumes a vital role in the analytical curricular sequence. According to stage level psychologists, experience is the catalyst for mental growth—providing that experiences are compatible with developed mental structures. For example, for the concrete operations level child, language curricular experiences may involve studying the conflict of responsibility by making an analysis of the conflicts of interest found in the book *Old Yeller* by Fred Gipson. In this story, concepts are presented concretely in a manner most transescents find interesting. In contrast, formal operations thinkers studying John F. Kennedy's *Profiles in Courage* are exposed to similar concepts presented in an interesting manner but also in a more theoretical context.

Another consideration for analytical curriculum development is including elements essential to stage level progression. The property of reversibility appears basic here. Mental stage level proponents recommend that a mental operation, in order to aid cognitive growth, should be followed by its reverse operation.

In the analytical curriculum, reversibility may be observed as a common element in all content areas. It is detected in mathematical processes; for example, the problem $52 \times 26 = 1352$ also may be inversely analyzed as $1352 \div 26 = 52$. In science, if one heats water steam is produced; inversely, if one cools steam, water is produced. Regarding language patterns, a student discovers in the phrase, "red house," that the object of description is preceded by a descriptive term; conversely, the transescent must reverse this pattern when examining the French structural expression, "maison rouge." Illustrations in social studies: youngsters learn that economic instability leads to cultural panic; and, inversely, economic stabilization eliminates this phenomenon.

A second mental process the architect of transescent curriculum must consider is that of associativity. This element permeates the total analytical curriculum. In a mathematical context, for example, the quantity $3 (A + B)$ may be analyzed for its variaous associations such as $3A + 3B$, $A + B + A + B + A + B$ or $A + A + A + B + B + B$. Likewise, an experiment in science viewing microscopic life involves factors in association such as stagnant water, food supply, and cell reproduction. Language areas provide similar associative patterns; for example, a paragraph consists of a main idea with subordinate elements in association. Within the framework of social studies, a culture may be considered as a totality—involving associative elements such as government, education, economy, and social institutions. Again, it is recognized that a mental thought process, in this instance, association, is a universal property found throughout the four content areas.

Increased academic excellence has become an integral part of American culture. Therefore, it is advisable to propose, approaches which accelerate mental stage development in the analytical curriculum at the same time being cognizant of the precarious emotional position of transescence.

The mental nature of the transescent learner offers a feasible alternative to this dilemma. While it is unwise for transescents to be expected to master a traditional high school mathematics course, some of the thought processes involved in advanced geometry courses can be grasped by transescents. For example, principles of projection, inherent in projective geometry, may be taught in the analytical curriculum, providing that they are presented through experiments commensurate with transescence. Similarly, the concept of probabilities, which is basic to the understanding of advanced mathematics and sciences, cannot be taught in a calculus approach; but it seems reasonable that a few of the foundation principles such as "chance" could be introduced to transescents through pertinent but mentally compatible activities. Also, the thought processes surrounding induction and deduction appear to lend themselves to transescent mental stages. For example, in a language context, a student might be asked to complete a plot of a story after being given only a few basic facts, such as characters, setting, and situation; conversely, a transescent may be presented with a story climax and asked to create all the associative elements leading thereto.

In this way, the analytical curriculum stresses thought processes which are within the mental capability of the transescent. As long as these analytical processes are presented on a level which can be attained by the tranesescent, emotional stress can become less of a significant factor and future learning of more difficult processes, if presented in the same analytical vein, can be accomplished more easily. Once again, the importance of appropriate stage level experiences in the development of mental structures is apparent.

In the analytical curriculum emphasis has been placed principally on thought processes. As such, the curriculum has been conceptualized within the boundaries of the general content areas of mathematics, science, language, and social studies. This approach is in contrast to the separate subjects found in the traditional curriculum, such as arithmetic, general science, spelling, penmanship, English, reading, foreign language, history, and geography.

Although it seems redundant to restate the basic premise for this decision, there are a few additional comments which merit mention: (1) Narrow segmentation reduces flexibility. Despite the fact that a student is avidly pursuing a profitable learning episode in geography, he must abruptly end this pursuit in order to move to an English class. By the time that geography period resumes the next day, much motivation has been lost.

(2) Narrow subject division means students often fail to integrate similar thought processes. To be worthwhile, learning activities should stress common thought processes. For example, since linguistic properties used in analyzing word structures are similar in reading, spelling, foreign language, and English, any or all of these areas can be utilized for this process.

(3) Students in the analytical curriculum should be evaluated on the sequential analytical concepts involved in their daily programs. Comprehensive examinations, which generally provide a major portion of a student's traditional subject grade in terms of passing or failing, are incompatible with the proposals made in this section. Evaluation should be concurrent in terms of individual progress in curricular aspects and may be reported to parents by means of progress check lists. Rigid pass/fail grading methods provide the transescent with considerable emotional pressure which is a detrimental factor.

(4) The schedule for the analytical curriculum should be flexible, enabling the staff to adjust to current changing transescent needs and interests. Adjustments and schedule alterations could be made during staff unit planning sessions and pupil/teacher planning sessions. As a series of illustrations: Figures 8 and 9 show a few of the vast number of flexible scheduling possibilities. In these illustrations, concrete level youngsters are symbolized as $C + 1$ and $C + 2$; formal operations transescents are listed as $F + 1$ and $F + 2$. In all sample cases, the schedules are geared to one-half of a total school day.

In Figure 8, the schedule provides for four equal time segments in a traditional type pattern. Probably this pattern would be used infrequently, since it schedules youngsters to meet with all four unit

CURRICULAR AREAS				
Mathematics	Science	Language	Social Studies	Resource
C + 1	C + 2	F + 1	F + 2	
F + 2	C + 1	C + 2	F + 1	
F + 1	F + 2	C + 1	C + 2	C + 1
C + 2	F + 1	F + 2	C + 1	

Figure 8. Analytical Equal Time Schedule.

members in one day. As such, it does not present youngsters with lengthy learning episodes. One deviation is noted: The C + 1 group, during one of the segments, is divided between a language learning episode and independent study in the resource center. There are occasions when this type of schedule could be advantageous, particularly for learning episodes which do not require experimentation, library research, or other time consuming approaches.

CURRICULAR AREAS				
Mathematics	Science	Language	Social Studies	Resource
			F + 2	C + 2
		F + 1		
	C + 2			
C + 1				F + 2
	F + 1	C + 2	F + 2	C + 2 F + 2

Figure 9. Flexible Analytical Schedule.

In Figure 9, considerable deviation is observed from the traditional pattern. Group C + 1 stays with the mathematics teacher for the entire session, while Group C + 2 devotes most of its time to science with a small segment of time in language and independent study. Formal operations Group F + 1 spends the greater part of the session in language study with the balance of time in a science pursuit. Group F + 2 divides its session time between social science and independent study under the direction of the resource person.

Of course, other schedule illustrations could be cited to demonstrate flexibility. One facet of flexibility, not illustrated by these samples, is the flexible nature of handling individual needs. In this respect even though Group C + 1 may be involved in a language session, the staff-student planning sessions may feel that certain individuals—for any number of cogent reasons—may profit more by following independent pursuits at the material resource center or perhaps by being a part of a group planning session. In such cases, these youngsters would not be part of the main group.

The socio-psychological model, described earlier, emphasizes the transescent's growing need for self-discovery and acceptance. Therefore, student participation in the planning of daily instructional activities becomes an important vehicle by which transescents' need for self-realization and self-acceptance is satisfied. The curriculum should not be considered as a means for imposing standards nor as a means for manipulating students toward these standards; rather, it should be viewed as a combined student-faculty planning effort set out to meet the challenge of middle school youth's educational and personal needs. In this way, the curriculum would continually be applying the principle of adaptability—an essential factor if transescents' rapidly evolving needs are to be successfully met.

In addition to the educational advantages of flexible scheduling, there are other concomitant values. Transescents are provided with opportunities for accepting personal responsibility vital to their evolving independence; they are able to pursue curiosity in an educational setting; and they benefit from the socialization made possible in the planning sessions held with their peers.

Middle School Grouping Considerations

Fundamental to the educational process is the grouping of students. Generally, youngsters have been educationally grouped according to a range of characteristics including chronological age, grade level, and/or some facet of intelligence. In any grouping philosophy there are inherent strengths and weaknesses; nonetheless, it is essential in a mass educational system that students be assembled in some manner for carrying on the educational process. The key question is, however, what means of grouping holds greatest promise in relation to the nature of transescence. In subsequent discussion, a proposed format for grouping will be explored. Essential grouping variables will be considered with suggested patterns offered for curricular and school grouping.

Close analysis of the socio-psychological model provides an awareness that there are certain variables which must be considered in transescent grouping. Physical characteristics, normally not considered in traditional grouping, cannot be dismissed—in view of the impact which changes in these characteristics have on the lives of transescents. If youngsters developed physically in a social vacuum, or in Samoa, physical change would matter little; however, it has been indicated that in our culture these developments create for the youngster changes in interests and attitudes having deep significance for transescent school associations.

Likewise, mental growth is an important consideration used in student placement. In this respect, the determination of the current level of cognitive development is the most plausible approach to using this variable. Utilized in this manner, mental growth stages are commensurate with the Geneva psychological viewpoint. Transescents grouped on this basis reflect a common educational base centering on current level of cognitive growth rather than on intelligence scores which provide a precarious and often misleading point of reference.

Cultural impingement on the transescent is a third major variable in grouping. Since anxiety and emotional stress have a marked effect on the progress of learning, a transescent's adjustment to diverse cultural forces, such as home stability, mobility, peer demands, or similar factors, cannot be disregarded. The changing interests and attitude patterns involved in transescent growth bear significance for student associations within the school society. Although in traditional educational grouping, heterosexual class combinations have been prevalent, interest patterns of transescents suggest that a same-sex arrangement may be used to advantage in the middle school.

Middle School Grouping Procedure

With a fundamental understanding of transescent environment, curriculum, and educational grouping considerations, it is now possible to suggest a middle school grouping format. Again, this grouping format is based on the socio-psychological model.

As transescents enter the middle school from the elementary school, each youngster will be evaluated as to his physical growth status and emotional characteristics. From a composite of characteristics, transescents may then be placed into base units, reflecting similarity of characteristics. Of course, as physical development and interest patterns change appreciably, alterations in school grouping may become desirable.

Within the framework of the base unit, transescents will vary as to their current stage of mental growth. This variance will necessitate having smaller internal groupings for instruction in the analytical curriculum. Based on reasons previously discussed, it is proposed that transescents be subgrouped into two levels: one level characterized by concrete operational processes and the second level reflecting the processes of formal operations. The transescents' mental growth progress will be constantly evaluated by the professional staff and adjustments will then be made commensurate with mental growth.

It has been noted that anxiety and emotional stress may have a marked effect on mental stage progress. Therefore, even though a student's mental stage development might place him into a formal operations level, emotional stress may hinder continued progress; thus, it may be in the best interests of the transescent to proceed in a less rigorous concrete operations context until the emotional crisis has passed.

The grouping mechanism for the physical-cultural curriculum involves associating youngsters from two separate base units. This procedure is necessitated by an analytical schedule pattern. Figure 10 depicts this arrangement.

SESSION	BASE UNIT A	PHYSICAL-CULTURAL UNIT	BASE UNIT B
A.M.	A + 1	A + 2 B + 2	B + 1
P.M.	A + 2	A + 1 B + 1	B + 2

Figure 10. Unit Schedule Pattern.

Figure 10 indicates that a physical-cultural unit is composed of transescents from two separate base units. Logically the physical-cultural combination should be derived from two base units of relatively similar physical and emotional characteristics.

While most transescents will spend three years in the educational model, exceptional youngsters may spend varying amounts of time in the organization. Staff evaluation may indicate on one hand that a transescent is exceptionally mature physically, mentally, emotionally, in peer interests and in associations. If so, it may be in the best interests of the transescent to be placed with students of compatible characteristics in the high school organization. Conversely, if these elements indicate an extremely immature status, it may be desirable for this youngster to stay in the middle school environment an additional year. It is strongly urged that *all* these described conditions exist before any fringe youngsters are assigned to an atypical sequence. This viewpoint further stresses that, as immature youngsters attain development, administrative flexibility permit these transescents to move at any time to an organization commensurate with their acquired developmental status.

Analytical Grouping

Research has been almost nonexistent on the placement of youngsters for instructional purposes relative to their stage level development. Now, a movement along these lines is underway. The results of this movement will fill a vital need. Flavell[1] comments on this progress:

> Piaget himself has never bent his talents towards making standardized intelligence tests out of the innumerable cognitive tasks he has created during his professional lifetime. But such an endeavor would surely be a logical extension of his work, and there is some activity in this direction. . . . One of the standardization projects is being carried out by Vinh-Bang and Barbel Inhelder . . . the other is going forward under Father Adrien Pinard. . . . The basic facts about the Geneva project are these. About thirty Piaget tasks drawn from various content areas (number, quantity, space, geometry, movement, velocity, time, chance, and others) were individually administered in standardized form to some 1500 children 4–12 years of age. The intent of the project appears to be to create a standardized developmental scale of reasoning and, in the process of doing this, to assess the validity of Piaget's conclusions about

---

[1] Flavell, *op. cit.,* pp. 361–362.

developmental stages, developmental interdependence of different cognitive acquisitions, and the like for those content areas studied. Although details are lacking the impression is that the outcome has been positive on both accounts.

It seems reasonable to assume that this research will continue to fruition. However, in the interim, a procedure for analytical placement will be suggested. In doing so, a review of the basic premise about stage level mental development is offered. This premise states that youngsters develop cognitive ability, as mental structures are created. Based on this position, it may be postulated that analytical curriculum content may be sequentially devised, founded on the stage characteristics of formal and concrete operations. By applying these characteristics, reported at length by the Geneva group, curriculum objectives may be constructed. These curriculum objectives could then be inserted into an evaluation instrument for statistical assessment.

The validity of this proposal may be questioned unless substantial controls are used. In this regard, it is suggested that both the basic curricular planning and the subsequent evaluation devices be constructed under the auspices of local educators in conjunction with professional psychologists who are knowledgeable in the stage level philosophy of Piaget. Certainly by combining the intellectual resources available in our universities with the pedagogical expertise of local educators, this task is surmountable.

As related previously, the emotional status of youngsters is a significant variable in grouping. In assessing this variable, educators may consult student records, former teacher comments, health records, and current suggestions from the professional staff. School placement may be adjusted in different ways. If the transescent's emotional problems are major, professional help may be sought with the cooperation of the home. If these disturbances are less serious but still influence transescent progress, study emphasis may be changed, thus reducing academic stress through some less rigorous mental pursuits until the temporary situation is righted.

Physical-Cultural Grouping

Transescent grouping for the physical-cultural curriculum will follow after an assessment is made of both the child's physical growth status and his interest patterns (evolving from physical development and cultural factors). Analysis of physical development should be based on information gathered from several sources.

In the middle school, the results obtained from transescent physical examinations are very important. In the traditional school, normally very little grouping use is made of physical examination data. However, in the socio-psychological model, research showed that there was a significant correlation between the onset of physiological change and skeletal growth. For example, it was discovered that most girls have their greatest height gain in the year preceding menarche. Researchers also indicated that trends in dentition and myopia accompanied the onset of transescence. Other scientists reported that as physiological changes occurred, changes in social interests and attitudes occurred.

As a result of a careful analysis of physical examination data compiled by competent medical and dental personnel, transescent educators now have meaningful ways of combining youngsters for physical-cultural activities. The physical-cultural curriculum is designed for maximum social interaction. If youngsters with radically different physical growth characteristics are grouped together, emotional stress will probably be heightened, due to incompatible characteristics and interests. The physical-cultural curriculum is the logical area where an understanding of growth changes vital for transescent emotional security can be centered; however, if girls who have not attained menarche are grouped with girls who have been menstruating for a long period of time, this advantage may be lost.

Information derived from physical examination data offers the educator "thinks to look for." It was stated earlier that physiological change is accompanied by an altered personal approach to life. Now educators, armed with the knowledge of the possible onset of physiological developments, may be prepared to adjust the educational processes as they occur. Normally, these adjustments would be made only after long periods of instructional frustration were experienced —this caused by ignorance concerning developing growth changes on part of the staff.

Transescent interests play an important role in peer associations. Transescents may often be observed associating with older or younger friends in play situations—again, substantiating in a subjective way, the reports of research scholars who have indicated that physical growth and interests occur irrespective of chronological age or grade level. Assessing this variable for grouping, transescent educators may employ a variety of sociometric testing devices. The results of this type testing may alter drastically as physical growth unfolds; logically, grouping patterns should alter accordingly.

A final consideration for grouping in the physical-cultural curriculum involves the sex of the transescent. In traditional schools, segregation of sexes for instruction occurs in several subject areas. It is suggested that grouping in the proposed physical-cultural curriculum be largely based on a same-sex nature. Of course, there will be some curricular occasions in which boys and girls may profitably integrate. For most physical-cultural curricular pursuits, however, it seems more reasonable (based on the characteristics elicited from the socio-psychological model) to conduct activities in a same-sex context.

Professional Staff Relationships

The curricular approaches proposed here imply altered professional staff relationships and responsibilities. In keeping with the philosophy of the analytical and physical-cultural curriculum, the following discussion will outline the professional staff's involvement in the middle school.

Physical-Cultural Staff. Staff members involved in the physical-cultural curriculum will include fine arts, practical arts, physical education, and cultural studies members. As a result of their preparation each of these teachers plays a vital role in the proposed unit approach.

The character of the physical-cultural curriculum in itself requires that faculty members approach their area of specialization broadly. These personnel are primarily agents for successful transescent socialization. Each of these transescent educators should have unique educational preparation and therefore should adequately instruct transescents in the skills of the various special areas. In addition to the academic teaching and equally important, the staff should be able to assist transescents in meeting the very difficult challenges involved in their growth processes. Moreover, the physical-cultural leaders have the opportunity to aid transescents in developing a cultural appreciation of the nation and the world in which they live. In the context of the interrelated unit, transescents have many opportunities to study, in a practical way, the lives of people whose culture is different from those in our society.

Analytical Staff. The professional staff members in the analytical curriculum include language, mathematics, science, and social studies teachers. Each of these specialists provide the analytical curriculum unit with specific content background as well as with a finite knowledge of thought processes involved in their area of specialization.

Although each of these areas is considered a separate analytical facet, the general emphasis placed on the universality of mental thought processes indicates considerable interrelatedness. There will be many occasions for each of these specialists to enter the content domain of his colleagues. For example, analysis of sound patterns in languages may be closely associated with the science of sound. Thus, when these faculty members plan content learning activities, they can at the same time work in close association with other content area specialists.

Resource Personnel. School districts have generally followed a pattern of promoting highly competent teachers to supervisory positions for the purpose of aiding teachers in the instructional processes. Although admirable in intent, there are often times when a dynamic teacher can become enmeshed in administrative detail by this pattern. As a result, students suffer from the loss of a highly competent professional. This is a particularly damaging situation because transescent educators who are highly competent are professionals possessing a keen awareness of the transescent's educational and personal needs.

A more beneficial solution would be to assign a master teacher to instructional level duties. This expert would, like the supervisor, have no specific teaching assignment but his abilities would be at the disposal of the unit. In one instance, he may act as a resource person for the other teachers by suggesting, upon request, teaching techniques which he has found helpful. At other times, he might work with a group of students who need special instructional help. By meeting with teachers in planning sessions, he could be of service by acting in liaison between the librarian at the resource center and the planning teachers. In general, however, his expertise as an educator would be involved with aiding the youngsters in a "grass roots" way, rather than by using another teacher as the vehicle to improve instruction.

These curricular approaches suggest the need for extensive faculty interaction when planning sessions devote their time to current and long range instructional objectives. In current planning, cooperation is particularly important in order to insure curricular flexibility. If a student is progressing well in one content area but poorly in another, or if a learning episode requires a lengthy time interval, current group planning may provide for these contingencies. Long range planning is equally essential to insure that there is instructional balance over the individual facets of the curricula.

CHAPTER VII

Guidance Services and Activities

Guidance is an important facet of the middle school program. The complex character of transescence requires that considerable guidance be given, if the multitude of adjustment problems facing transescents are to be met. In this regard, the transescent educational planner has primarily two decisions to make: (1) what is the function of the guidance service, and (2) what is the role of the counselor within this function. In this chapter, these fundamental issues will be analyzed as applicable to transescence, and proposals which seem to be most compatible with the characteristics of transescents will be suggested.

The guidance function is most logically considered an integral part of the total educational program of the middle school. By creating an environment, a curriculum, and grouping procedures commensurate with the characteristics and needs of transescence, an educator is in reality creating a school which is based on using guidance. It seems reasonable to make the statement that a school which programs in such a way as to reduce emotional stress aids in reducing the number of student adjustment problems. Certainly, it would be naive to assume that in our culture student problems will become extinct through school organization; nevertheless, one may argue that transescent problems can be curtailed through appropriate educational programming.

Based on this philosophy, the fundamental core of counselors in the middle school should be the instructional staff. Boys and girls encountering emotional problems due to atypical growth patterns should be aided in meeting these concerns first and foremost by the school personnel with whom they are most intimately associated. The socio-psychological model indicated that in the past transescents have not placed much faith in teacher help in this regard. Likewise, in the earlier model, research studies indicated that most youngsters have had very little school assistance in meeting the challenges provided by their growth processes. It is, therefore, suggested that transescent instructional personnel should assume the basic responsibility when it comes to guidance, rather than relinquishing this professional service to a corps of counseling specialists.

Even though total effort is made in the instructional lives of transescents, there will be some youngsters whose problems are so deeply rooted that normal efforts fail. Here a counselor's services are needed: (1) by means of individual conferences and maximum personal interest, a counselor may be able to help the transescent over difficult emotional hurdles; (2) through many meetings and consultations with the troubled youngster, the counselor may suggest alterations in the student's educational program; and (3) if all of these efforts fail, the counselor may take the initiative and refer the ill-adjusted student to personnel or agencies of greater competence.

Related Guidance Programs

The guidance function should in a practical sense be an integral part of all school activities. An illustration of this philosophy can be found in socialization programs. These programs should be devised and based on the characteristics, interests, and social needs of transescence. The remainder of this chapter will be devoted to suggested formats for such activities.

The first of these proposed activities, the Social, should be scheduled periodically throughout the school year. The Socials should be planned and conducted by transescents with the advice of the professional staff. Such planning should involve all details of the activity—theme, decorations, activities, entertainment, and refreshments.

In creating the program for the Social, total participation of all transescents should be stressed as opposed to a boy-girl, couple-type relationship characteristic of high school socials. Group activities such as large circle mixers, square dances, and games, such as table tennis and shuffleboard, should predominate. Through this approach, socialization of the majority of transescents whose interests are of a same-sex nature would be enhanced. At the same time, there should be some opportunity for opposite-sex peers to associate informally.

Another suggested segment of the Social are "vaudeville" type activities. Performing acts, such as singing, dancing, and playing instruments, are particularly appropriate for middle school youngsters. Since many transescents are quite competent in this area, but rarely have an opportunity to display this competence before an audience of peers, this approach provides the youngster with an opportunity to gain such peer respect.

There are several guidance-related advantages in this type event: (1) It provides the transescent with needed socialization opportunities in an atmosphere reflecting little social pressure; (2) it provides transescents with opportunities to assume responsibility and leadership since they are included in planning the program, decorating the physical area, rehearsing, performing acts, selling refreshments or some other activity; (3) the Social provides means whereby transescents who do not excel physically or academically can gain peer approval and respect.

A second proposed guidance program is an Interest Activity Program scheduled as part of the school day. In this program, a wide range of interest activities can be conducted. Again, students, in association with faculty members, would be responsible for planning and conducting the program.

A gamut of activities can be devised, based on student interests and suggestions. This program might include any of the following types of activities: social work group, such as the Junior Red Cross; nature programs, such as a botany nursery; physical activities, such as games and intramurals; mathematical activities, such as surveying; science endeavors, pursuing rocketry or model airplane construction and operation; quiet activities, such as chess; fine and practical arts group activities in arts and crafts; social science endeavors, such as reenactment of famous battles; language activities, such as dramatics or newspaper publication. There are, of course, many other diversified interest activities which may be suggested by the transescents themselves.

In the Interest Activity Program, emphasis should center on activity rather than on club-type procedural meetings. Activity emphasis is preferred since transescents require considerable physical exercise and peer interaction. Often in the "meeting" approach, these essentials are absent. It is further suggested that this type program be scheduled midway in the school day in order to take advantage of the physical and emotional relief inherent in these type activities at a time of day when the need for release is most necessary.

The Interest Activity Program seems to offer transescents the following significant guidance-related advantages: selection of an activity based on personal interest; involvement in activities which are physical in nature; increased experiences beyond those in the basic curricula; ease of association with peers in an informal, creative atmosphere; exploration of interests which logically form the foundation of later careers.

A third suggested guidance related program is a Student Association composed of elected student officers and representatives. The purpose of the Association would be to provide a democratic forum for student discussion and debate concerning current school affairs, problems, and issues. School wide officers for the Association should be nominated, campaign for election, and be elected as part of a total school effort. Local constituencies for the Association would be the homerooms in which various student problems could be discussed. Discussion topics often range from school issues, such as the advisability of the school adopting a Korean foster child, to personal areas such as manners, family relationships, or school behavior. Representatives from each of the homeroom constituencies would be elected to serve in the Association.

The Association provides guidance benefits for the transescent, since it presents an opportunity for students to weigh alternatives and make decisions in responsible situations. Furthermore, students are able to conduct Association work under an adult mandate based on trust. The emancipation process dependent on gradual acceptance of mature responsibility is enhanced through this activity.

A fourth proposed guidance-related activity is a Student Service Committee. Students serving with this committee would have diverse responsibilities. One segment of this group could be responsible for providing public service announcements via the public address system or school bulletin board. (These announcements may range from reading an inspirational message to reporting yesterday's intramural results.) Another segment of this committee could be meeting, in association with faculty members, to plan, schedule, or conduct school assemblies. Other students in the Student Service Organization could act as school receptionists, office helpers, or ushers for auditorium programs.

The Student Service Committee potentially provides transescents with several guidance benefits. First, students are given the opportunity to assume leadership in important school functions. Secondly, transescents, through planning sessions with adults, receive a genuine feeling that their actions are essential to successfully carrying out important functions. Thirdly, transescents are provided activities compatible with their interests and developmental needs.

CHAPTER VIII

Administration

This chapter will stress administrative considerations regarding the models described in previous chapters. Emphasis will be focused on the central school district administration's responsibility regarding the middle school. In this context, the segments of this chapter will include staff-personnel relations, school-community relations, physical plant, fiscal affairs, and evaluation. Proposals in each of these facets will be limited to those areas considered most pertinent to this project.

Staff-Personnel Relations

Educational progress cannot be accomplished solely by organizational mandate regardless of its organizational compatibility with student characteristics. Ultimately the gain to be accomplished is in human relationships. That is why the means whereby the professional staff conducts the educational process is of such importance.

Recruitment of personnel is a key factor in developing a successful middle school staff. Because transescents have unique needs, this endeavor takes on particular importance. Fundamental to the acquisition of a competent staff is an understanding of the character and goals of the school in relation to a potential staff member's personal and professional qualifications. Since the nature of the proposed middle school has been described at length, the focal point here will center on what characteristics transescent educators should possess.

The prospective teacher of transescents should have a thorough professional preparation. This background training should give the teacher an extensive understanding of both the physical and mental growth processes of transescence and particularly an awareness of these growth patterns in relation to our culture. The teacher's educational preparation should provide competence in a subject area— this competence should include not only a comprehensive knowledge of subject content but also a knowledge of the function of the thought processes relative to the area of specialization.

The socio-psychological and educational models imply what personal characteristics are necessary for an educator of middle school youth. Like all educators, these teachers should be healthy, vigorous, and intelligent. Beyond these general traits, however, there are other essential elements listed here in the following non-preferential order:

Personal Security: The insecurity of transescents requires daily examples of adults who exhibit confidence and faith in themselves.

Understanding: As the emancipation process develops, teachers may be of help to youth by being good listeners and by showing an interest in students.

Resourceful: It has been suggested at length that experiences are crucial at this age group. A teacher must not only be aware of this need, but also should cognitively react in a divergent manner in providing the diversity of needed experiences.

Adaptability: Being able to continually alter one's daily schedule is a necessary quality for middle school teachers. An inflexible person who depends on routine for personal security probably will find the proposed educational model frustrating.

Enthusiasm: Transescents profit from an enthusiastic adult. Teachers who are cynics will tend to stifle rather than motivate curiosity necessary for learning experiences.

Cooperative: In the educational model, stress was placed on interrelatedness of curricular content and flexible scheduling. The points will require considerable faculty interaction.

Sense of Humor: Teachers who fail to see the humorous aspects in daily human involvements may find difficulty in relating to transescents.

Even though this list of characteristics is far from exhaustive, it does provide a basis for qualifications to be considered in the selection of teachers for this age grouping.

Another staff-personnel consideration revolves around the ratio of male to female members on the staff. It was suggested in the socio-psychological model that, in our culture, the frequent absence of the father has a decided effect on the transescent. In this regard, a faculty composed mostly of women may not provide the youngsters with adequate opposite-sex adult involvement. It is particularly important to secure male personnel to fill this need.

The transescent educational model has implications not only for the acquisition of competent personnel, but also for the successful assimilation of these members into the school complex. Often new staff members have difficulty in adjusting to a school. These problems emanate from a variety of sources, but, relative to the transescent school proposal, there are certain suggestions which appear to be particularly necessary. First, since the school has many flexible features, incoming faculty members should receive a thorough orientation about the goals and features of the middle school program. Secondly, because some of these procedures are different in substance from those of the traditional school, it is essential that a comprehensive series of in-service meetings be held to insure that the faculty understands the goals and processes of the program. If ill-informed, a faculty member's morale and personal contribution can be seriously impaired.

Similarly, the placement of faculty members into curriculum units is an important consideration. In the process of individualizing student programs, developing curricular content, or evaluating student progress, considerable faculty interaction will occur. An administrator, thoroughly acquainted with faculty personalities, should be able to arrange teaching units in a manner that major personality differences are avoided.

Playing a vital role, the administrator of a transescent school should have exceptional competence as an instructional leader (with all of the implications this term suggests) and, in addition, must have a sincere personal interest in students. Transescents are at a point in their development when they demand more than organizational ability from an administrator. In every possible instance, he should associate with the student body. This does not infer that he must become a part of the transescent subculture, but his physical presence and his interest in them as individuals should be evident to transescents. This association helps the administrator become cognizant of the needs of the educational process. Such an awareness insures that educational change will not come from a "detached" office.

Little comment has been made here concerning the importance of non-professional personnel. As essential as these employees are just for the efficient operation of a school, they often make significant contributions far beyond their basic responsibility. An understanding secretary, a custodian, or a cafeteria worker sometimes helps a transescent over a difficult temporary hurdle. Therefore, selection of these workers should be given careful consideration.

School-Community Relations

Within our American society, interest in children's education is pervasive. Thus, when restructuring the school's traditional format, an exhaustive effort should be made to interpret these changes to the citizenry. When planning a drastic change, such as taking sixth grade youngsters, normally associated with elementary school, and combining them with children usually considered secondary students, an interpretation to the public seems particularly essential, for it is only natural that children and their parents are concerned about this change.

High priority should be given to the transescent so that he fully understands proposed alterations. A carefully planned series of small group meetings in which staff members discuss the many various facets of the middle school should take place. During these sessions, every attempt should be made to explain the purposes of the new organization as well as its characteristics. Particular emphasis in areas which will be different from those of the elementary school is required. In subsequent years, after original implementation, youngsters entering the middle school should spend an orientation day in the new school. During this visit, they may attend classes, talk with teachers, view slides of the features of the program and, in general, gain a practical knowledge of their future environment.

Prior to initiating a middle school, educators should provide opportunities, by means of all available media, for parental understanding of the nature and goals of the restructured organization. In these attempts stress should be placed on the changing socio-psychological characteristics of children. Through these interpretive occasions, parents can be informed about the impending organizational change and then they will be able to make any necessary mental adjustments to the new concept. These interpretive efforts should be made well in advance of actual change. With community support, the proposals contained in the educational model will have greater possibilities for success.

When the transescent school becomes a reality, the school's obligation for concurrent interpretation of all facets of the school program remains a necessary component of school-community relations. This effort will require a variety of communication approaches: small group discussions relative to various educational segments; large group parent-teacher educational meetings; written correspondence; and, informational releases by mass media.

A special function, suggested by the socio-psychological model, is having the school serve as a resource center for parents. Vital to the emancipation process, which often presents both youngsters and parents with anxiety, is that parents have a clear understanding of transescence. A parent resource center containing filmstrips, professional periodicals, pamphlets, and source books could prove exceptionally helpful to the interested parent.

School-community relations are to be viewed in both directions. The community can aid the school in significant ways. Communities may do many things to assist in creating favorable staff morale beyond those of economic support. Since transescents need adult relationships based on security and ease of association, the community can offer diverse activities establishing rapport and mutual respect. In turn, staff members develop the security necessary for successful relationships with transescents.

Physical Plant

To facilitate and accommodate the educational process, a school plant cannot be merely a building and grounds. Indeed, the educational home of transescents should enhance curricular accomplishment. Since middle school curricula emphasizes flexibility, individualized instruction, and independent study, the physical environment should reflect this philosophy. Classrooms need be adaptable in order to provide for varying class sizes, group activities, and to offer opportunities for varied experiences. All physical facilities should provide functional arrangements in such a way that students may use these facilities with relative ease in a manner commensurate with educational pursuits.

Mental growth is heavily dependent on experience and the physical plant should provide maximum experiential opportunities. For example, since it appears more beneficial to study mitosis by means of a microprojector than by vicarious means, this equipment should be provided. Classrooms should be equipped as completely as possible with those things necessary for the student to attain experiences associated with the content field being studied. Moreover, the resource center should be more than just a reading library; it should be an experience center where the students can listen to music or to taped messages by means of individual listening devices. It should offer facilities for viewing slides, filmstrips, or television. In addition to a quiet study area (such as reading stations), a section should be provided where a group of students can get together to verbally discuss research projects they are undertaking.

Inasmuch as experiences should not be limited to mental growth processes, there should be outdoor physical plant facilities providing for physical education activities as well as areas for nature projects, nursery activities, wildlife study, and conservation. There should be indoor physical facilities, too, allowing for a wide diversity of physical activities included in group and individual sports.

A fact to be considered is that transescence is a dangerous time of life; youngsters at this stage of development tend to be awkward and many times excitable in their personal actions. Quite often, this eagerness excludes their taking contemplated safe courses of action. This combination of conditions frequently results in accidents. To offer protection, therefore, school facilities should be designed (or altered) to provide maximum safety factors. Railings, safety glass, wide corridors, fire escapes, strategically placed sidewalks and bicycle traffic lanes—all should be studied and set up to meet and even go beyond state and local regulations. Although economy is necessary in school plant development, transescent school safety features should not be austere.

On the whole, the middle school plant should be aesthetic. The age group, with its multitude of potential emotional stresses, benefits from cheerful and attractive surroundings. The interior of the school plant should be painted in color schemes which are warm and relaxing. The various segments of the building should be well lighted and maintained in such a manner as to insure cleanliness. Similarly, exterior physical facilities should be attractive.

Fiscal Considerations

The educational model suggests effects on school financing. A discussion of school fiscal affairs implies that there is more to it than just a financial accounting in school operation. Rather it should be regarded as the vehicle through which a middle school serves youth Thomas[1] philosophically writes in this regard:

> A school budget for most people in its usual form is mainly a set of figures. It will be unfortunate if you think of a school budget only in terms of money. The prudential approach to the analysis of this chart for financial action is important; however, the budget plan is much more than graphs, tables and charts. Primarily, it is a human document. There are many stories and many dramatic incidents within its framework. It tells of fine people devoting their lives to young people to insure that our society will be a better place in which to live. It tells of teachers working to make young people happier, to prepare them to meet more adequately the many complex tasks before them, and to be as self-reliant as possible.

Hopefully, it is in the spirit of this quotation that financial support for meeting transescent developmental needs occurs. Commensurate with this purpose, the following are expenditures suggested by the educational model.

A primary concern is what effect a realignment of youngsters into a different housing arrangement will have on school district finances. In many instances, by placing youngsters normally associated with Grades 6, 7, and 8 into a separate housing unit, the elementary school population will be smaller and the high school student body larger. Depending on the local school district status, the realignment will alter district financing to a varying degree. In rapidly expanding districts, little added expense need be incurred. Conversely, in stable population areas, increased cost may occur if there is a need for plant alterations.

Within the framework of the middle school model, there are

---

[1] Maurice J. Thomas, "The Real Meaning of a School Budget," *School Fiscal Problems and Procedures* (Pittsburgh: University of Pittsburgh Course Syllabus, 1964), p. 21.

several proposals which might effect expenditures. One area is related to the idea of offering maximum opportunities for educational experiences. Although many learning activities may be conducted with little expense, the proposals for increased indoor and outdoor science laboratories and for increased use of instructional aids would tend to expand cost. Also, there would be additional expense for transportation to such experience centers as conservatories, museums, and planetariums. Conversely, a large expenditure for the creation of a foreign language electronic laboratory is not recommended.

Since the educational model has proposed curricular and guidance arrangements which vary from the traditional, a slight increase in professional staff members, stemming from greater emphasis on individualized instruction and the institution of resource teachers, would probably be forthcoming. Based on the proposals made in the educational model, it is suggested that approximately 56 teachers, 3 administrators, and 2 counselors be employed for a middle school student body population of 1,000. This total of 61 staff members per 1,000 students compares favorably with the recommendations made by McKenna.[2] He cites a national staffing range of 25 staff members per 1,000 students to 90 members per 1,000 students with a current national average being 45 members per 1,000 students. McKenna declares an optimum staffing ratio of 68 staff members per 1,000 students.

Added cost might be involved also, if nonprofessional employees are added to help with the routine procedures of the educational process. Curricular proposals would necessitate developing curriculum materials for the various segments. Since this type of project requires considerable professional effort, it is unlikely that these programs could be effectively conducted during the school year; thus, a team of staff members working during the summer months would entail added expense. Decreased expenditures suggested by the educational model would be involved in the reduction of guidance and administrative supervisory personnel.

Provisions for physical activities will influence spending. It has been suggested that interscholastic athletics not be part of the physical development program for transescents. Although a well directed

---

[2] Bernard H. McKenna, *Staffing the Schools* (New York: Bureau of Publications, Teachers College, Columbia University, 1965), pp. 7–8.

intramural athletic program would involve some financial expenditures, the cost of interschool competition tends to be appreciably higher. Here, cost of transportation, equipment, and salaries would not be a major expense.

Expenditures for the physical plant would no doubt remain compatible with present outlays; however, there are some exceptions which would require additional cost. These exceptions, related to the need for flexible classrooms, for instance, would include items such as movable partitions, and similarly, would require the constructing of listening booths and small projection rooms in the resource center.

Because of the vast number of intangibles involved in these fiscal considerations, it is not possible to predict specific budget figures that would be necessary to carry out the proposed transescent educational model; nonetheless, it seems reasonable to suggest that the conceptualized educational model will require a greater per student expenditure than is currently involved in the education of transescents.

Evaluation

Evaluation is a vital part of educational administrative procedure. Throughout this writing, the fundamental elements of transescent behavior were analyzed and ways pointed out for incorporating them into an educational organization. Validity of the conceptual rationale and the functional model can only be determined by applying scientific inquiry to the middle school after it becomes a reality. Ultimately a definitive appraisal of the multitude of facets involved in the educational model will be required. Here only the broad substantive areas associated with determining operational success can be listed for consideration in the evaluation process.

An essential area for evaluation: the suggested change in the pattern of school district organization. The creation of a middle school naturally alters the elementary and high school units. Under this proposal, the elementary organization would exclude the sixth grade, while the high school would return to a four year status. In each case, a systematic appraisal of these organizations would be necessary. While the evidence presented in the socio-psychological model justifies the middle school concept, an appraisal is needed of present elementary and high school units and their comparative values.

Another significant consideration for evaluation: the attitude of transescents toward the middle school concept and processes. Transescents are a part of a culture which has been viewing the junior high school as a maturity symbol. Therefore, middle school students initially may feel that a lack of participation in senior high activities is detrimental. This point of view should be analyzed, as it has implications as to whether the middle school concept will be accepted or not.

Evaluation of the middle school should, further, include: an analysis of transescents in their educational setting. The socio-psychological model indicates that the characteristics of students in grades 6, 7, and 8 form a theoretical basis for a middle school; subsequently, the middle school educational model that evolved was based on this rationale. Scientifically, this concept can be objectively confirmed only through research studies involving transescents in a middle school as compared with similar students in a traditional elementary or junior high school unit. It is in this way, that the validity of middle school relationships involving physical growth status and evolving personality and interest patterns can be ascertained.

A logical area for comparative analysis: the status of transescent emotional problems in the conceptualized middle school contrasted with those in the traditional school organization.

In the middle school model, a restructuring of educational processes founded on the nature of transescence was undertaken. Since proposed curricula were devised to meet the needs of transescents, it is believed that the educational progress of these youngsters, in relation to the present demands of the culture, will be enhanced; furthermore, this improvement should come about with a minimum of emotional stress on the learner. Since it is believed that transescent educational achievement will be improved by centering instruction on mental thought processes involved in broad content areas as opposed to a pattern of individual subject fields, these proposals should be tested in the practical functioning of the middle school.

Considerable emphasis has been made that a flexible learning environment is the most suitable climate for transescent development. In a traditional sixth grade elementary setting, flexibility permitting interaction among students with comparable physical and social characteristics is not possible. This situation opens the way for making a sharp evaluative contrast between the students in an elementary unit and transescents in a middle school. A similar-type comparison can be made between transescents in the middle school and transescents in the junior high school.

The educational model includes provisions for students to proceed through the middle school with grouping and advancement based on physical, mental, emotional, and social characteristics. This proposal was made irrespective of an age level or grade level; in addition, this provision enabled students who were exceptionally early or late in maturation to spend an inordinate amount of time in the middle school. Heretofore educational policy provided for atypical sequences, usually based on mental ability. These patterns oftentimes resulted in undesirable social and emotional effects on personality development; therefore, the educational model proposes to reverse this pattern and place major emphasis on the physical, social, and emotional concerns when grouping transescents. This is another area to be evaluated after the educational model is put into operation.

Other areas for analysis and evaluation: (1) Teacher participation in the educational model. The suggested patterns of teacher involvement are somewhat atypical, and they should be evaluated in relation to the vital concerns of staff morale, teacher understanding of transescence, and faculty interaction. (2) Community reaction. The attitude of parents who have viewed the junior high school as an integral part of the American education system has implications for the successful development of the middle school concept. While it is essential that the professional staff program educational policy, the stand made by the citizens of a community toward educational policy is fundamental. In this context, educators must evaluate the reaction the community makes to a program which is contrary to tradition and the implications the reaction has on the reorganization program.

CHAPTER IX

Conclusions and Recommendations

In this chapter, conclusions and recommendations, formulated upon the basic assumptions of this study, will be presented.

The assumption that physical maturation is occurring at an earlier chronological age in our culture is accepted. Research studies reported in the socio-psychological model clearly indicate a discernible trend in this direction. In actuality, the socio-psychological model presented evidence that this trend has developed to the point where transescents with similar physical maturation characteristics are now being educated in two separate organizational levels—the sixth grade, considered elementary, and the seventh and eighth grades associated with the junior high school.

Although the current 6-3-3 grade organization effectively met the needs of youngsters in the earlier decades of this century, it no longer relates realistically to physical characteristics of transescents. Moreover, the socio-psychological model indicates that the basic cause for the earlier physical maturation trend has been a favorable socio-economic climate. Since this factor continues to become more and more favorable, the strikingly earlier physical development trend no doubt will continue. Unless there is alteration of the educational grade organizational sequence, the present disparity between student characteristics and the educational organization will widen.

The assumption that earlier physical maturation is accompanied by earlier social interest patterns in our American culture is substantiated. The socio-psychological model indicates that the physical maturation process is conditioned by the American culture. Research studies, which were reported, consistently showed a significant correlation between the level of maturation and social interests and peer involvement patterns. As a result, transescents not only mature physically at an earlier chronological age, but they also develop earlier social peer interaction patterns. Again, this has deep implications for transescents in an elementary setting, or for adolescents in a transescent grouping. In both cases, peer associations are not compatible.

The assumption that present graded school groupings are incompatible with the diverse characteristics of transescence is substantiated by the data presented in the socio-psychological model. Within its framework, there are definite indications that youngsters develop toward maturity irrespective of grade levels or chronological age. In effect, it has been shown that there is no stereotype for levels of human growth. Our culture, as a matter of fact, often expects different actions from two transescents even though they might be the same age. Since transescents of different ages and grade levels often exhibit similar characteristics and needs, the present educational attempt to place transescents in a grade level according to chronological age cannot be defended. Acceptance of this assumption indicates that transescents should be grouped for instruction according to individual maturational status, rather than age or grade level.

The assumption that present elementary and junior high schools do not realistically reflect students' current maturational patterns is substantiated. The socio-psychological model provides research evidence that students presently placed in a sixth grade elementary setting possess much greater similarity of physical maturation and social interests with seventh and eighth grade students than they do with children in grades kindergarten through five. For similar reasons, this same phenomenon of earlier physical maturation and social interest patterns suggests that it is inadvisable to place most present ninth grade junior high school students with the transescent grouping. The ninth grade student reflects physical, mental, and social characteristics appreciably more advanced than middle school transescents.

The assumption is substantiated that the school, as an agency of society, does not now reflect contemporary cultural status of middle school students. The socio-psychological model presents extensive research evidence that by the nature of American culture the length of time which a youngster spends in childhood has been reduced. While this reduction stems from earlier physical maturation attributed to socio-economic factors, the significant increase in experiential opportunities for today's youth adds to the situation. In other words, the development of earlier interest patterns is associated both with earlier physical maturation and with increased experiences afforded youth in our culture.

Despite extensive documentary evidence to the contrary, adult members of society, particularly educators and parents, have not accepted earlier maturation trends, and, in fact, offer a counter-force to their existence. In this regard, the socio-psychological model indicates that parents reared in an earlier cultural era do not accept youngsters' earlier emancipation efforts. In a similar way, it is observable that educators have maintained school organizations, educational processes, and teacher preparation programs geared to characteristics of youngsters of a previous era.

More and more professional literature is offering evidence that the junior high school concept is being seriously challenged. Usually, however, the suggested remedies take the form of treating the ills of the present structure rather than proposing an attack at the root causes of the problem. Substantiated assumptions of this study indicate that the root of the problem be attacked—through an altered school district organizational pattern—that an elementary unit of grades kindergarten through five, a middle school grouping of grades six through eight, and a high school unit of grades nine through twelve, be initiated.

Based on these conclusions, it is recommended that school district building programs include the construction of new plants and/or alterations of existing plants in order to facilitate putting the middle school philosophy in effect. It is recommended further that school district expenditures, designated for the creation of a middle school, be commensurate with the educational requirements of this particular facet within the total program.

It is also recommended that state departments of education recognize the middle school concept (1) by altering state reimbursement formulas to help meet increased costs, and (2) by devising certification standards for teachers serving this level. It is vital for institutions of higher education to create programs designed to prepare teachers and administrators specifically for the middle school. Preparatory courses stressing the nature of transescence and the interrelatedness of transescence and our culture should be emphasized.

This monograph has created a functional model for a middle school commensurate with available knowledge derived from the related academic disciplines of psychology and sociology and the foundations of education and educational administration. It is hoped that many scholars will consider the basic premises offered, evaluate their worth, and use them in whatever way will be most beneficial in educating today's children.

Glossary

1. *Culture*—the total environment to which the human organism interacts.

2. *Developmental Growth Characteristics*—the changing nature of the human organism as it grows to maturity.

3. *Diverse Relationship*—the range on a continuum of a human characteristic or action.

4. *Idiographic Relationship*—the effect of the individual on the social system.

5. *Middle School*—a school unit which follows the elementary unit and precedes the high school unit; includes students from grades six, seven and eight of a graded school organization.

6. *Nomothetic Relationship*—the effect of the social system on the individual.

7. *Nongraded School*—a school in which students' progress is related to personal characteristics rather than to age or grade level.

8. *Transescence*—the period in human development which begins in late childhood prior to the onset of puberty and extends through the early stages of adolescence.

Bibliography

BOOKS

Allport, Floyd H., *Theories of Perception and the Concept of Structure.* New York: John Wiley and Sons, Inc., 1955.

Brodbeck, May, "Logic and Scientific Method in Research on Teaching," in *Handbook of Research on Teaching,* ed. N. L. Gage. Chicago: Rand McNally and Company, 1963.

Bruner, Jerome S., *The Process of Education.* Cambridge, Mass.: Harvard University Press, 1962.

Coleman, James S., *The Adolescent Society.* New York: Cromwell-Collier Publishing Company, 1961.

Davis, Allison, "Child Training and Social Class," in *Child Behavior and Development,* eds. R. G. Barker, J. S. Koumin, and H. F. Wright. New York: McGraw-Hill Book Company, 1943.

Davis, Kingsley, "The Sociology of Parent-Youth Conflict," in *Social Perspectives on Behavior,* eds. Herman D. Stein and Richard A. Cloward. New York: The Free Press of Glencoe, Inc., 1958.

DeYoung, Chris, and Richard Wynn, *American Education.* New York: McGraw Hill Book Company, 1964.

Flavell, John, *The Developmental Psychology of Jean Piaget.* New York: D. Van Nostrand Company, Inc., 1963.

Gesell, Arnold, Frances Ilg, and Louise Ames, *Youth, The Years from Ten to Sixteen.* New York: Harper & Row, Publishers, 1956.

Griffiths, Daniel E., "Some Assumptions Underlying the Use of Models in Research," in *Educational Research: New Perspectives,* eds. Jack A. Culbertson and Stephen P. Hencley. Danville, Ill.: The Interstate Printers and Publishers Inc., 1963.

Havighurst, Robert J., *Developmental Tasks and Education.* New York: David McKay Company, Inc., 1952.

Havighurst, Robert J., and Bernice L. Neugarten, *Society and Education.* Boston: Allyn and Bacon, Inc., 1957.

Horrocks, J. E., *The Psychology of Adolescence.* Boston: Houghton Mifflin Company, 1962.

Inhelder, Barbel, and Jean Piaget, *The Growth of Logical Thinking from Childhood to Adolescence.* New York: Basic Books, Inc., 1958.

Jersild, Arthur T., *The Psychology of Adolescence.* New York: The Macmillan Company, 1963.

Kuhlen, Raymond G., *The Psychology of Adolescent Development.* New York: Harper & Row, Publishers, 1952.

Mead, Margaret, *Coming of Age in Samoa*. New York: William Morrow and Company, 1928, 1955, 1961.

Parsons, Talcott, "The Kinship System of the Contemporary United States," in *Social Perspectives on Behavior,* eds. Herman D. Stein and Richard A. Cloward. New York: The Free Press of Glencoe, Inc., 1958.

Prescott, Daniel A., *Factors That Influence Learning, Horace Mann Lecture, 1958.* Pittsburgh: University of Pittsburgh Press, 1958.

Stolz, Herbert R., and Lois M. Stolz, "Adolescent Problems Related to Somatic Variations," in *The Forty-third Yearbook of the National Society for the Study of Education,* ed. Nelson B. Henry. Chicago: University of Chicago Press, 1944.

Strang, Ruth. *The Adolescent Views Himself, A Psychology of Adolescence.* New York: McGraw-Hill Book Company, 1957.

Tanner, J. M., *Growth at Adolescence.* Oxford: Blackwell Scientific Publications, 1962.

Toby, Jackson, *Contemporary Society.* New York: John Wiley and Sons, Inc., 1964.

Tyler, Ralph W., "The Contributions of the Behavioral Sciences in Educational Research," in *First Annual Phi Delta Kappa Symposium on Educational Research,* ed. Frank W. Banghart. Bloomington: Phi Delta Kappa, 1960.

ARTICLES AND PERIODICALS

Harris, Dale B., "Sex Differences in the Life Problems and Interests of Adolescents, 1935 and 1957," *Child Development,* XXX (1959).

Inhelder, Barbel, "Some Aspects of Piaget's Genetic Approach to Cognition," *Monographs of the Society for Research in Child Development: Thought in the Young Child,* XXVII (1962).

Lounsburg, John H., "How the Junior High School Came to Be," *Educational Leadership,* XVIII (December, 1960).

Meredith, Howard V., "Stature and Weight of Children of the United States with Reference to the Influence of Racial, Regional, Socio-Economic, and Secular Factors," *American Journal of Diseases of Childhood,* LXII, November, 1941).

Parsons, Talcott, "Age and Sex in the Social Structure of the United States," *American Sociological Review,* VII (1942).

Ramsey, Glenn V., "The Sexual Development of Boys," *American Journal of Psychology,* LVI (1943).

Reichert, J. L., "Competitive Athletics for Pre-Teen Age Children," *Journal of the American Medical Association,* CLXVI (1958).

Stone, C. P., and R. G. Barker, "The Attitudes and Interests of Premenarcheal and Postmenarcheal Girls," *Journal of Genetic Psychology,* LIV (1939).

Index

Index

A

Abel, Theodore M., 18
Activity Program, Interest, 88
Allport, Floyd H., 4
Ames, Louise, 8, 42
Analytical Curriculum:
  associativity, 73
  equal time schedule, 76
  experiences, 72
  flexible schedule, 76
  language, 66, 73
  mathematics, 66, 73
  science, 66, 73
  social studies, 66, 73
  staff members, 84
  thought processes, 66, 72, 75
Angelo, Henry, 20, 52
Athletics:
  effect on physical development, 22
  interscholastic, 22, 59
  intramural, 59
Aub, J. C., 11

B

Barker, R. G., 20
Bayley, Nancy, 20, 34
Benedict, Ruth, 51
Boas, F., 11
Brodbeck, May, 5
Bruner, Jerome S., 28, 38
Burton, Rodger V., 47

C

Clements, E. M., 11
Coleman, James S., 54
College preparatory courses, 63, 74
Conjugal family:
  emotional effect, 46
  in America, 43
Cultural relationship and:
  changes in America, 53
  emotions, 17, 48
  experiences, 32, 33, 53
  physical development, 9, 20, 22, 41,
    42
  social implications, 17
Curricula structure, Middle School
    (Schema), 65

D

Davis, Allison, 32
Davis, Kingsley, 45
Davis-Thomas, E., 11
DeYoung, Chris, 35
Dinitz, S., 46
Dollins, Joseph, 20

E

Educational model, 66
Egocentrism, 36
Emancipation:
  parents' role, 44, 45
  process, 43
Espenschade, Anna, 10
Evaluation of middle school concept:
  attitude of transescents, 100
  community reaction, 101
  school district organization, 99
  teacher participation, 101
  transescent reaction to middle school,
    100, 101

F

Faust, M. S., 20
Fiscal considerations, 97–98
Flavell, John, 26, 27, 28, 29, 30, 31, 32,
    33, 34, 36, 37, 80
Fort Couch Middle School, 2
Frank, L. K., 21

G

Geneva Group, 25, 81
Gesell, Arnold, 8, 42
Glueck, E. T., 46
Glueck, S., 46
Gould, H. N., 13
Gould, M. R., 13
Gow, Jr., J. Steele, 16, 53
Greulick, W. W., 10
Griffiths, Daniel E., 3, 5
Grimes, Ethel, 14
Grouping:
  base units, 79
  mental growth characteristics, 79
  physical characteristics, 78
  same-sex pattern, 79

Growth trend:
  affected by:
    climate, 15
    nutrition, 16
    race, 15
    socio-economic conditions, 16
    temperature, 14
  earlier onset:
    height and weight, 10
    menstruation, 10, 12, 13
    myopia, 11
    teeth eruption, 11
Guidance counselors:
  instructional staff's role, 86
  specialist's role, 87
Guidance function, 86
Guilford, J. P., 37

H

Hall, G. Stanley, 2
Harris, Dale B., 49, 51
Harrison, R., 21
Havighurst, Robert J., 3, 21, 33
Hellersberg, E., 21
Higher Education Institutions, 104
Holzner, Burkart, 16, 53
Homework, written, 60
Horrocks, J. E., 22
Howe, Paul, 16

I

Idiographic, 6, 7
Ilg, Frances, 8, 42
Inhelder, Barbel, 27, 29, 32, 35

J

Jersild, Arthur T., 12, 35
Joffee, Natalie F., 18
Jones, Mary Cover, 18, 19, 20, 51
Jones, R. Stewart, 48
Junior High School:
  challenges to, 104
  effect of changing culture, 2
  philosophical base, 1

K

Kuhlen, Raymond G., 9, 12, 44, 51, 54

L

Landis, J. T., 50
Latham, A. J., 20

Learning climate, flexible, 58, 60, 63, 64
Lee, B. J., 51
Levy, David M., 46
Lounsbury, John H., 1

M

Machover, K., 21
Maturation:
  emotional and social implications, 17
  emotional effect on boys, 18
  emotional effect on girls, 19
  interest patterns, 20
McCord, Joan, 47
McCord, William, 47
McKenna, Bernard H., 98
Mead, Margaret, 40, 41
Mech, Edmond V., 20, 52
Melby, Ernest O., 57
Meleney, Helen E., 10
Menarche:
  emotional effects, 18
  earlier onset, 12, 13
Meredith, Howard V., 10
Meyer, William J., 50
Mills, C. A., 10, 14
Model:
  definition, 4
  isomorphic relationship, 5
  model relationship (schema), 6
  socio-psychological model (schema),
    6
More, Douglas M., 19
Murray, E., 46
Mussen, P. H., 18

N

Nathanson, I. T., 11
Neugarten, Bernice L., 3
Nomothetic, 6, 7
Norder, H. Orville, 55

P

Parsons, Talcott, 43, 46
Peake, Charles H., 55
Pendleton, William C., 16, 53
Physical-Cultural curriculum:
  cultural studies, 66
  equal time interval schedule, 68
  fine arts, 66
  flexible schedule, 69
  physical education, 66
  practical arts, 66
  staff members, 83

Physical-Cultural grouping:
  interests, 82
  physical examination, 82
  same-sex, 83
Physical-Cultural unit, 67
Piaget, Jean:
  accelerated learning, 32
  background contribution, 23
  balance and equilibrium, 27
  characteristics of learning philosophy, 34
  egocentrism, 36
  experience, 33
  functional invariants, 31
  intellectual development, 27, 30, 32, 35
  mathematics and science, 26
  motivation, 33
Pickett, K. G., 11
Puberty, 8
Prescott, Daniel A., 23, 37
Punke, H. H., 44

R

Radler, D. H., 44
Ramsey, Glenn V., 11, 15, 52
Reckless, W. C., 46
Reichert, J. L., 22
Remmers, H. H., 44
Reporting to parents, 71, 75
Resource Center for Parents, 95
Resource Personnel (Supervisors), 84
Riesman, David, 49

S

Samoan culture, 40–42
  American culture comparison, 41, 42
  cultural-growth patterns, 40
Sarnoff, David, 53
Scarpatti, F. R., 46
Scheduling of students:
  equal time interval schedule, analytical curriculum, 76
  equal time interval schedule, physical-cultural curriculum, 68
  flexible schedule, analytical curriculum, 76
  flexible schedule, physical-cultural curriculum, 69
Schiller, Marie, 16
School-Community relations, 94
School District Organizational Pattern, 104

School plant:
  aesthetic importance, 97
  educational characteristics, 95
  experience opportunities, 96
  outdoor facilities, 96
  safety features, 96
Service Committee, 89
Shonfeld, W. A., 19
Simmons, K., 10
Smith, W. M., 50
Socialization programs, 87
Socio-Psychological Model, 7
  based on literature, 5
  curricular structure (schema), 65
  relationship to educational environment, 58
  relationship to educational model, 65
Social system, 3
Spaulding, C. B., 42
Staff, non-professional:
  importance of, 94
Staff, professional:
  administrator's role, 93
  characteristics, 92
  in-service training, 93
  placement, 93
  preparation, 91
  recruitment, 91
  resource personnel (supervisors), 84
Stages of learning:
  characteristics:
    accommodation, 31, 60
    adaptation, 31
    assimilation, 31
    conservation of mass, 27
    reversibility, 25, 28, 73
  concrete operations, 25–26, 61
  effect of experience, 32, 33
  egocentrism, 36
  formal operations:
    definition, 28
    grouping, 79
    propositional thinking, 28, 29
  grouping, 79, 80
  preoperations, 25
  sequence of development, 29, 30
State Departments of Education, 104
State Department of Education, Pennsylvania, 2
Staton, Thomas F., 17
Steiner, M., 21
Stolz, Herbert R., 8, 9, 19
Stolz, Lois Meek, 8, 9, 19
Stone, C. P., 20
Strang, Ruth, 7
Streams, Carl R., 2

Student Association, 89
Sutherland, Ian, 15
Symond, P. M., 52
System Theory:
  definition, 3, 4

T

Tanner, J. M., 9, 11, 12, 13, 15, 16
Tasch, Ruth J., 35
Thomas, Maurice, 52, 97
Thurber, Emily, 47
Toby, Jackson, 21, 43, 47, 48
Towne, L., 11
Transescence:
  definition, 3
  democratic attitudes, 63
  fads in dress, 55
  geographical mobility, 54

  interests, 51
    earlier development, 53
  peer relationship, 48
  sexual development, 11
  socio-economic class effect, 47
Tseng, S. C., 49
Tyler, Ralph W., 4

U

Upper St. Clair, Pennsylvania, 2

W

Whitacre, Jesse, 14
White, William H., 54
Whiting, John M., 47
Wilson, Dagmar, 15
Wynn, Richard, 35